Gentle Spirit

Gentle Spirit

Alan Ames

ISBN 978-0-9820329-1-6

Dedicated to:

Chaldean Catholic Archbishop
Paulos Faraj Rahho of Mosul,
killed in Iraq march 2008 R.I.P.

Contents

Preface

IN THIS BOOK the Holy Spirit has given an insight into His love for mankind and in His love He guides people to live the way that is best for their whole being. It is shown how life can be lived to the full joyfully in His love and how love of others helps bring joy into the lives of others and into a world so full of misery. The Holy Spirit explains how mankind was created in joyful love to live happily with God forever. That this is possible for all people to achieve by God's grace if they so desire and make the effort to live as He asks. The truth of mankind is revealed exposing the weaknesses and the strengths of people, both of which can become blessings if used in the right way.

Every page is full of the gentle love of God which is encouraging, offering forgiveness and offering hope in Him. The Holy Spirit opens up the spiritual and mystical to explain to mankind what is truly happening in life both on the physical and spiritual levels. He shows how each person is under constant attack from evil and how each person is offered by Him, the grace needed to overcome evil in their lives and in the world. Every word in this book is given by the Holy Spirit either directly or indirectly through His guidance which was asked for in prayer before each of the letters written, or the interviews given.

As you read the messages, you will see some have scriptural references, while others have none. This is because in the beginning the Lord did not give me any references, but from December 1995 the Lord began to do so at various times. When I am given the references from Holy Scripture, it may be one or two lines, or only one or two words from a line. Sometimes two or three lines from different parts of Holy Scripture are combined to make the reference. The references at first were taken either from the *Jerusalem* or *Douay-Rheims Bibles*, but later to avoid any confusion, my spiritual director and I decided to use only the *New American Bible* for references.

From The Holy Spirit

THE TWO GREATEST COMMANDMENTS

THE TWO GREATEST COMMANDMENTS seem to be the hardest for people to follow and the easiest to ignore: "You shall love the Lord, your God, with all your heart, with all your soul, and with all your mind." This is the greatest and the first commandment. The second is like it: "You shall love your neighbour as yourself." The whole law and the prophets depend on these two commandments (Matthew 22:37–40).

So often people see so little in these commandments because they seem so simple yet these are what the faith that The Lord, Jesus, gave us is built upon. These two commandments are so deep and mysterious that a person in this life on earth could never come to understand them fully. So many Christians however tend to just pay scant attention to these commandments and look past them for something that they believe is more intellectually stimulating, or more exciting, or more mysterious.

How foolish it is to do this, for in these two commandments the mysteries of the faith can be opened and more clearly understood and in the excitement of this knowledge the soul is stimulated and led to reach higher spiritual levels. It is in loving God with the total self, the total being, that the soul is filled with grace that enables it to experience the glory of God's love for the person.

As the soul is glorified in the love of God it is raised up, drawn closer to God and as this happens the glory of God's love begins to radiate from the soul. In this state the whole being is now drawn to God in thoughts, in words and in actions as now the spiritual, mental and physical person becomes one, totally focused on God and freed from the chains of the world. In this state the desire of the entire self is to please God and to serve Him in love. In this state the worries of the world subside as the person begins to realize that all of their life is in God's hands. That there is nothing the world can do to them unless God wills it or allows it to happen for the sanctity of the person, and also maybe for the sanctity or salvation of others.

With this knowledge comes a yearning that only God's will be done, regardless of what it is, for now it is seen that whatever happens truly is a blessing from God.

Understanding this brings a person to hunger for God's blessing in all they do, knowing that any crosses they may carry or any suffering they may endure are not curses, are not punishments from God, but are signs of God's love for them as He allows them to become true imitators of His Son, Jesus Christ.

It is in this true imitation of Jesus, The Lord, that each person can be then led to perfection as they are lifted up through, with, and in Christ to higher levels of grace. It is in this imitation of The Lord, in the difficult times as well as in the good times, that the person is molded to become the holy person they were created to be, the holiness that is only found in true love of God and of fellow man. It is through this complete acceptance of God's loving will the person removes all the barriers between them and God as they are brought to the sublime holiness that life is meant to be lived and experienced in. In this holy state then every moment of life opens up to reveal the glory and grace of God within it. Now every moment is a moment of experiencing heaven on earth as the glorious love of God embraces the person who in love of God has given their all to Him.

With this embrace the eternal joy and bliss of heaven fill the mind, the heart and the soul. Now there is no misery in life, now no suffering is too great, now no chains can bind the person as now the person is totally free of the bondage of the world and is free in the grace of God. It is in this state that the presence of The Divine One, Jesus Christ, is truly felt as the kingdom of God is revealed in Him in all its glory.

It is as the person lives this way that their life is now lived on two plains at the same time. One is living, walking and breathing on the worldly plain. The other is where the inner self is living on the heavenly plain close to God and close to all the residents of heaven. These two plains, two worlds, now become one in the person so that whomsoever they come in contact with notice the love, the peace, the holiness that God has bestowed upon the person. Now also through the one who lives in this state

17

God pours out the grace that the world needs, the grace that brings the world a little closer to God as it changes lives by touching hearts and souls. Through the person, by the grace of God, heaven's embrace is felt by the whole world even if people do not see or understand this, for much is happening in realms beyond the vision of man. Now the person becomes a true vessel of grace and a magnifier of grace, as God in His wisdom and love uses the individual as a channel through which to reach out to the troubled world both on the physical and spiritual level. God uses the person to bring balance back into an unbalanced world. On the physical level God's grace and love, united in the love of the individual who has totally given themself to God, pours out to heal, to comfort, to bring peace and hope to a confused world. On the spiritual level God reaches out to bless souls, to caress souls and to fill souls with the grace and the strength they need to love Him and to live to His way. As God, through the vessel of love, touches the souls of others He draws them out of the dark and into the light of His divine love and in doing so weakens the grasp evil has on the souls of all mankind.

As all this is happening the one who has become a vessel of grace and love is opened by God to receive even more grace and more gifts for the good of mankind. With the continued total commitment to God by the person there is a never ending flow of grace from heaven to earth, a river flowing from the heart of God through the person to wash the world in grace. It is then that the individual is lifted higher and higher, drawn closer and closer to heaven and becomes like a citizen of heaven walking on earth.

This has been seen in the lives of the great saints, where so many miracles happened because of their holiness and total commitment to God. As with the great saints a person who is living this way sees now that in their love of God the love of man is entwined and that the more they try to please God and serve Him the more God uses them for all of mankind. Now a burning desire grows within to love all people and to serve all people because it becomes clear that God loves all people and that God has and continues to serve people because He loves them. Now no longer does the person look upon others and judge them by their physical appearance or what they have or who they are, for now all are seen as equal. All are seen as treasures of God's love, all are seen as brothers and sisters and all are seen with eyes and a heart that desires only the best for them and that will do all it can, by the grace of God, to help each person discover the full truth of God. Each one is now seen in the beauty of the love of God in which they were created and now in each person is recognized a masterpiece that the Divine Master has gifted the world with.

Seeing with eyes of grace it becomes clear that there is a great harvest of love that God wants brought home to Him and so there grows within the desire to work tirelessly in bringing the souls of others to God in love. As the grace of God strengthens and drives the person on, the one who is living completely for God now becomes a gatherer of souls. With every soul brought to God the desire within burns stronger and stronger to bring these gifts of love to Him. No matter how much the person works, no matter how many souls are touched it is never enough, for the person feels within that if one soul does not feel the touch of God's love then there is a soul that may be lost to the dark and the thought of that brings such anguish. No matter how heavy the crosses are, no matter what opposition they face, no matter what it may cost them, even their life, the servant of God continues on in love.

When they feel tired they find themselves renewed in God in His holy presence in the Eucharist. When they feel they cannot go on they find that God's grace lifts them beyond thoughts of self to thoughts of God and of others. Then they realize how they must always keep looking beyond self and beyond the world. How they must keep looking to heaven so as to let that heavenly grace, that heavenly love and that heavenly world elevate them above the physical plain to the mystical plain and in that plain let the mystical love of God, through the Eucharist, envelope them, protect them and guide them to fulfil God's will in their life. Now with fervent love the person works all the harder in physical ways when needed, by helping those in need, the poor, the lonely, the suffering. In spiritual ways through prayer, through the absorption of the Holy Word of God in Holy Scripture and the sharing of that Holy Word and through the offering of the power of the Sacraments for the good of others. In the mystical by reaching out from deep within their soul beyond words, beyond thoughts but with the innermost being begging God for His Mercy for others, even the worst of sinners, and allowing God to lift the soul up to Him in this cry of love. As they are drawn up by God, in this moment of grace, there is no desire to be drawn up alone but the desire that all people should join them. As God opens up His mystical heart in love the person does not want to enter it alone but wants all others to join them and so the person calls louder and louder from their entire being for God to grant all people the grace to enter His loving heart.

20

The ecstasy that now is experienced is filled with also a sadness that not all share in this divine gift of joy. Now agony and ecstasy are united because of the knowledge that souls will be lost by their own free choice and the knowledge that souls will be saved by the love of God. The agony opens up the sight to what is happening in the spiritual realm as God allows the person to see how evil is at work in destroying souls. Now it is seen while God's workers are harvesting souls in love, at the same time the evil angels are working to harvest souls in hatred, in selfishness, in greed and in sin and the acceptance of it. Then the ecstasy opens up as the Angels of God become visible standing beside each person there to protect them, to care for them and to guide them. Now there is a knowledge that each person needs to embrace God's angels so as to be kept safe from harm.

As the spiritual realm opens up all the servants of God on every level are seen working hard to bring souls home to heaven. Those alive on earth, those who have gone to heaven and those who have always been in heaven are united as one great army of love fighting to bring souls to God. It is also seen that this army of love needs willing recruits who are prepared to live the pure and holy life that God calls people to through His only Son, Jesus Christ, because those who join the dark in its fight for souls are many, even though some do not understand what they are doing. Some do not understand that anytime a person leads another into sin, into doing what is wrong they become joined with the evil angels in the destructive work of evil and they join in the fight against good.

Looking into the spiritual realm and looking upon the battle that is raging with the spiritual sight and the mystical wisdom that God bestows, it becomes clear that to defeat the evil ones, sacrificial love, goodness and purity are needed. These are the weapons that God gives to overcome even the fiercest of evil ones. It is when people stand firm in these that the power of Christ's victory on the cross pours out through the person. It is clear that sacrifice is needed for it is in each loving sacrifice that true love is seen and the sacrifice of Christ, The Lord, is revealed again and again. It is in sacrificial love that the barriers of self are removed so as to let the free flow of God's divine grace through. The power of goodness is realized as the person now sees that goodness is an impenetrable barrier against evil. Every act of good counteracts every act of bad. Every act of good opens up souls to the grace and love of God. Every act of good touches all of mankind and reduces the effect of evil upon it.

As the impure acts of evil come into sight showing how they hurt mankind by drawing it deeper into depravity, immorality and darkness, the awareness of how important purity is becomes obvious. Purity is seen for what it is a sword of pure light that cuts through the darkness and disperses the dark to reveal souls to the perfect love of God. In the presence of pure sacrificial love evil cowers as the power of good forces it back from where it came, it flees back into the abyss.

It is no wonder evil attacks these wonderful ways and confuses people into thinking that those who embrace sacrificial love, goodness and purity are to be scorned, mocked and rejected.

Looking into the spiritual realm by God's grace, it is seen that at each moment there are souls ascending to heaven and souls descending to earth. Those who have lived for God ascend the ladder to heaven while those who are yet to live on earth descend into the bodies that

God in His divine love has created for them. Lights of love ascending and descending. Joy fills the heart as the person realizes they are seeing saints on their way home to heaven and future saints in the making. Watching the souls descending to earth and seeing them enter the creation of life in the womb God has made, through the union of man and woman, brings great hope that each one will become the person they are meant to be. Then to see so many of these new beings destroyed in the womb by the foolishness of mankind and to watch as the evil ones laugh at this great slaughter fills the one graced by God with the burning desire to confront this great evil. To see heaven shedding tears at the destruction and rejection of God's gifts saddens the soul and draws it into a union with all of heaven in a cry for justice. Then seeing how, as those young ones who have not been slaughtered enter the world, from the very first heart beat, from the very first breath the battle for their souls begins. Watching as the guardian angels stand by each one's side to protect them from harm and watching how foolishly often the parents do nothing or little to protect their young from evil and so make the work of the guardian angels much more difficult. Then God, through His gift of spiritual sight, allows the person to see how many of the young do not have the stain of original sin washed away by the divine grace of God in Baptism and so are left weakened against evil and opened to evil. To see that many are not given the loving guidance needed to recognize sin and to reject it. To see how many of the young who are drawn into sin are not told of or do not understand the grace there for them in the sacrament of reconciliation where the Holy Spirit through the priest removes the stain of sin from souls, purifies the soul, and opens the soul to grace.

To see whole lives wasted in sin and in self, through the deceptions of the evil ones, makes the heart and soul ache with grief as those lives end and the souls begin their descent into the darkness of hell. Watching the souls sinking into the dark the one with spiritual sight now experiences agony realizing what will happen to these lost souls. The person now cannot stop the love within from imploring God to have mercy on even the worst of sinners and in true love begging God to send them to hell in place of those who are being lost. Every soul is seen as precious and the thought of just one being lost causes immeasurable suffering, so in an act of love the person is willing to sacrifice for the sinners being taken to hell; sacrifice their entire self. This is now a mystical imitation of Christ who in His sacrificial death descended into the depths to release souls from hell. Now, united with Christ, by His grace in His sacrifice, there is no longer a fear of death and hell but only a desire to do whatever is necessary to save souls from the torment of hell even if the person would have to endure that torment themselves. It is in this moment the full force of hell attacks as the evil one does not want any soul taken from him. The person may be assailed by evil both spiritually and physically. However there is nothing evil can do to deter a person who has reached this spiritual level by the grace of God, as now there is no fear of evil and only complete trust in the love of God. Now the person knows they are secure and that unless God wills it, so that souls can be saved, there is nothing evil can do.

If there is any pain or suffering it is welcomed as it is recognized through this God is pouring out the grace of salvation. If there is any torment God is thanked over and over for the blessing bestowed on the person that allows them to suffer for others. The soul cries out joyfully "Victory" knowing that the victory of Christ is truly being realized in and through them. While evil howls in despair as the sacrificial light of Christ burns brightly in the soul of the person and disperses the dark around it. How evil despairs as true love confronts it. The true love of God and the true love of man united in willing and true sacrifice. Sacrificial love which by the mercy and grace of God is more powerful than anything that evil can muster. It is when a person truly reaches this state of love that sanctity is theirs by God's grace. This is the state many martyrs reached and in this state of holiness gave their lives willingly for love of God and love of man.

Now with this spiritual awareness it is seen that there are realms of light and of dark and that sitting in between these realms is the earth and those on it.

How the world created from the light of God to exist in His light is being slowly enveloped by the dark. There is around the world a blanket of greyness which becomes darker and darker each time someone sins and accepts evil into their lives. However, through this mist of sin and evil there are lights shining brightly burning through the smog of corruption. So many intense lights joining to be one as they shine forth from every tabernacle and from every Holy Mass from the Body, Blood, Soul and Divinity of Jesus Christ, He who is light, the eternal light present in every Eucharist. Other less intense lights are also shining through the blanket of grey from the lives of those who love, serve and obey The Lord God, Jesus Christ, the children of light, with each of these lights melting away the evil around them as they join becoming one in the Lord of Light. In response from the depths of the darkness a web stretches out in a desperate attempt to trap the world and drag it into the pit of hell. With so many people willingly grasping on to this web because of their pride and weaknesses. People who are caught like fish in a net, a net which is emptied into the inferno of suffering that awaits within the dark.

GOD FIRST IN ALL THINGS

THE HEARTS OF many today are closed to the fullness of God because so many of even those who attend church are only opened in the way the person wants them to be and not in the way God wants them to be. Many seek God with their own personal agenda which in their lives is placed before God's agenda for the person. This in itself is a large barrier between God and the person, the barrier of pride.

To overcome this barrier each person needs to turn to God and ask His Holy Spirit to help them place God first, to place God before self. It is in doing this, with the true desire to love God more, that the person then allows the Holy Spirit into their life as master not as servant. In bowing to God in this way the heart and soul are opened by the Holy Spirit to accept the fullness of God's truth and the fullness of God's love. When this is done then no longer does the person have any doubts in God's love for them. No longer does the person have any uncertainty in life as now the grace of God fills the being with the security of His divine love. The truth of God becomes clear and no longer is there any crisis in faith as the person knows God is real and God does care for them. Now with the heart and soul opened by the grace of God life changes completely as life is now always seen as a blessing no matter what happens and each day is lived to the fullest in love of God and of others.

Now church life changes so that no longer are the Sacraments, Holy Scripture or prayer seen as duties or routines. Now church life is filled with excitement as the person realizes through the church they can come closer to God in the spiritual acts and spiritual exercises they do.

Now in every church celebration of the sacraments joy is found as it becomes clear that the grace of God abounds in each one. Each sacrament now shows the person clearly the depth of God's love in these wonderful blessings He gives. Now the sacraments are recognized for the jewels of love that they are and are embraced in love as the Holy Spirit opens the person to the grace and blessings in each sacrament. It is then by God's grace that life comes into true perspective and the heart comes to know that life is empty without God and that life is only lived to the fullest in Him.

The things of the world are no longer of prime importance as their true value is seen now in respect to God and eternity. The things of the world no longer trap the person as they are set free by the Holy Spirit from the prison they had placed themselves in through focusing on the world and its temporary delights. The eternal gift of God's love is raised on high in the person's life becoming the reason for living as it is meant to be. The heart and the soul long only for God and yearn to be closer and closer to Him and the joy of His love. The person has the longing to be with Him in heaven in their innermost being. In this state the fear of death is gone for now death is seen as the doorway to heaven through Christ, The Lord, and there is no doubt in this divine truth.

All this happens because the person invites the Holy Spirit to help them in placing God's will first before their own and asks the Holy Spirit to help them to open their lives to God and not rely on themselves to do so. The cry "God first in all things" becomes their cry. In this cry is an expression of the soul's true love of God which lifts the soul heavenwards as it reaches out for God to fill it with His love and in response to this cry God pours out

His divine love in an embrace of heavenly glory. In this embrace the soul dances for joy as all it could ever desire and so much more fill it and satisfy it. In this embrace the Divine One raises the soul on high to experience another facet of His love because now God's will and the person's will are one in love, and God's will, which is supreme love, envelops the humble soul in the eternal symphony of love shared with all those who have accepted God's will in their lives before their own.

Within this symphony there is a song of hope as the words of Jesus, The Lord, are echoed in love "Thy will be done on earth as it is in heaven". The importance of these words becomes clear as now the person realizes this is the way anyone can find heaven by living on earth to God's will so that in death they are taken into the divine will of God in heaven. It also becomes obvious that if people on earth will alter their lives and live to the will of God instead of their own will that the world will change to be paradise once again. That by living to God's will heaven will be there in the people's lives as they become one in the divine will of God. This is how heaven comes to earth and this is how the world is changed for the better. It is man's will that separates heaven and earth and it is God's will that reconciles and unites them. It is the submission of mankind's will to God's will that restores the balance that God created all in; the balance of love. Evil works on the pride of people to persuade them to believe that their own will should be first in all things and that God's will, while nice, is just theory or ideals that people may try to live to but really cannot or do not need to and so they should not make too much effort to do so. Foolishly many are drawn into this prideful way and because of this are drawn into sin or the acceptance of sin.

If man's will is supreme then anything can be justified even the worst sins, no wonder the world is in such a terrible state. The will of man has brought chaos, destruction, wars, immorality and selfishness. Yet people still believe in the will of man before the will of God and so the suffering continues. God's will is love, goodness, peace and joy. However, this does not seem to be enough for mankind or is not as appealing as the wicked ways of evil. Mankind's pride has taken it away from God and mankind's blindness keeps it away.

There is no need for mankind to fear God or His judgement if they have lived as best as they could to His will. The only fear should be the suffering a person invites upon themselves by the rejection of God's will or the placing of one's own will before God's. God has made it clear from the very beginning that He loves mankind and only wants the best for it. Mankind though seems to ignore or not believe in this divine truth and prefers to accept the evil one's deceit which has been shown from when Adam and Eve first sinned to bring only hurt. How blind mankind has become, that even as it looks back upon history and all the suffering within it, the mistake of turning from God is not learned from. It is obvious that man's history would have been one of joy, happiness and peace if God's will had been accepted and embraced. However, because God's will has been rejected so often, instead of all the goodness that could have been there is misery and pain. God's will is that all people live happy lives on earth in Him and find eternal joy in heaven with Him. God does not desire that any soul would go into eternal suffering but He does allow people to have the free choice to decide where they want to go. This free choice is a great sign of love from the Divine Master who says in this granting of free will, "Love me but do so freely and willingly". To do anything less would make mankind's relationship with God one of authoritarian master and slave rather that one of father and child.

With this freedom God also gives all the direction mankind needs to live as it should. He directs mankind in His Holy Word, in His prophets, in His Holy Catholic and Apostolic Church and in the greatest gift of love in His only Son, Jesus Christ's life on earth. Even when mankind strays God does not give up in trying to bring people to happiness and home to heaven. He reaches out each moment in love calling all to repentance and to the acceptance of His forgiveness and divine mercy. Even until the last breath of life God offers, in His immeasurable love, each one the chance of coming home to Him. Sadly so many refuse His continuous offerings of mercy, forgiveness and grace because they have allowed themselves to be blinded to the truth of God and His divine love. In this blindness of pride people even ask why God would send anyone to hell, not seeing it is a person's own actions and choices that send them there. Not seeing it is because of putting the world and its ways before God and His ways that is the reason some people go to hell.

How the evil one laughs at the foolishness of so many people who reject what is good for them and accept what is bad for them. So many who then in their pride denounce those who live to God's way and will not believe there is anything wrong in the sins the many commit and there is no price to pay for sinning. So many who do not believe in God and so see no reason not to sin or no reason to behave in a good way, thinking that those who do know God and believe in Him are crazy. The truth is that it is the non-believers who are crazy to risk their very souls for a few years of self indulgence and sin on earth which may cost them an eternity of self-induced suffering in hell. It is pride that unites mankind with evil while it is true humility that unites mankind with God and it is pride that takes many to hell while true and humble love bring many to heaven. Pride, Lucifer's sin passed on through Adam and Eve to mankind but overcome in the humble love of Christ, The Lord, and in Him the victory over sin passed on to mankind in the lives of all who truly follow Him.

Submission Of Will

Just as the Lord Jesus, submitted completely to the will of The Father all who follow Him are meant to submit to the will of God in imitation of Him. It is in the total abandonment of self into God and into His holy will that a person opens themselves by their free will to becoming vessels of His love. In this submission to God's holy will a person removes all barriers between them and God by God's grace and permits God to possess them completely and to use them completely for His glory and for the salvation of mankind. It is also in this complete submission of will that a person overcomes the great sin of pride which first caused Adam and Eve to sin as they put their desire and their will before the will of God. In this humble giving of a person's will to God evil is rejected and overcome as God's grace fills the person with the holiness of His love. Now in every moment God's will reigns supreme and so there is no room for evil to enter into the life of the person.

It is in this replacing of one's own will with the will of God that a person reflects the life of Mary, the mother of God. Mary completely gave herself to God and accepted His will over her own regardless of what it may cost her, even if it cost her life. Mary knew in her heart and soul that no price was too high for living to God's will as she knew that it is for God, in God and with God we are created to exist. So to deny His will in life would be to deny the eternal truth of existence. Mary knew that in the total giving of self to God that she pleased God and because she truly loved Him this was a consequence of that love. Mary held nothing back from God and gave back to Him what he had first given to her; herself. The world could do nothing to stop Mary for she desired only for God's will to be done and she knew His will was far greater than anything of the world. She also knew that no matter what happened to her if it was God's will it would bring only love, grace and goodness into the world. In the total giving of her life to God and the total submission of her will to God, Mary showed all humans it is possible to live completely for God. Mary, the greatest human created by God, created to be the vessel through which God would come to earth but still created with free will which she freely returned to God.

Anyone who will submit themselves to God's will as Mary did will find holiness as Mary did. While it will not be the same level of holiness that Mary achieved still it will be a holiness that lifts the person to eternal love in heaven. This lifting can occur in life as well as after death as in the total submission to God's holy will a person resides as the citizens of heaven reside and so a touch of heaven is in the heart and soul and the kingdom of heaven has a home in the life of the person. Just as in Mary's case this then becomes obvious in the way the person lives, avoiding and rejecting evil at all times and exuding true love and holiness where ever they go.

A person's will becomes a holy will when they freely and in love give their will to God and ask Him to replace their will with His holy will. It is in doing this that a person can become a saint of today on earth and can join the Holy Ones in heaven as an eternal saint.

THE LIGHT

THE LIGHT CAME into the world so that darkness could be overcome and so that people could be set free from the prison of darkness mankind has placed itself in. From the very first moment on earth The Light shone brightly burning away the darkness and replacing it with the illumination of divine love for mankind. The dark tried to overcome The Light from the moment it was revealed to mankind. However, nothing the dark did could extinguish The Light, could cover The Light or could reduce The Light. The Light which is Jesus Christ, The Lord, glowed in His heavenly glory on earth and all who would look with open hearts saw this glory. As The Light drew more and more people into its glorious love the dark responded in hatred and anger doing its worst to destroy The Light. While some who were first drawn to The Light would falter in pride and in self others would give their all to remain in The Light for now they knew the glory of God. While the darkness could seduce the weak away from The Light and into the shadows the truly strong remained in the glow of heavenly love and desired only to humbly serve The Light by being vessels of divine love going out to all in the hope of bringing their brothers and sisters out of the fog of evil and into the Sonshine of love.

As they did this the darkness of evil sent all its forces against them in an effort to stop The Light spreading but those who clung to the glory of God in love, in trust, and in faith would not falter. The Light itself was assailed and in what seemed like a victory for evil The Light was put to death. Some who looked upon the suffering Lord saw only defeat and believed no more. Some who looked upon the suffering Lord thought The Light was dying. Some who looked on the suffering Lord mocked Him as they let the darkness envelop their hearts and souls. However, The Light was not to be denied and through the suffering, through death and through the grave The Light was resurrected to continue pouring out its eternal rays of love. In this final victory over the darkness of evil The Light swept away evil's hold on the world and set the captives free so that anyone who sought to live in The Light with a true heart would never be enslaved again.

In this eternal moment The Light reached out from the beginning of time until the end of time and released souls from their torment to bring them into the never ending joy of God's love. In this eternal moment the fallen of the dark were shown the power of The Light of God, the power they could never overcome. In this eternal moment Lucifer screamed out in anger and torment at his defeat.

He Is Risen

THE LIGHT WENT into the darkness of death and illuminated that dark so that captives could be set free. Death was overcome by The Light and The Light shone brightly and The Light was not diminished by the darkness.

The Light was and is Jesus Christ, the eternal light of God. The Light which can shine brightly in every life. The Divine Light that is there for all. The Divine Light who waits in love and hope for people to invite The Light within. This invitation should be a genuine one where the person is prepared to help overcome and remove the darkness within their life. Where the person is prepared to sweep clean their heart and soul, by the grace of God, so that there will be nothing in their life to block The Light.

It is then when The Light comes into the life of a person that the dark in their life is illuminated and sometimes for the first time the person sees how the dark has overshadowed them and taken them away from The Light of life. It becomes clear how even the smallest sin brings the shadow of evil into a life, a bad thought, a bad word or a bad action. It becomes clear how these small sins lead a person further and further away from The Light and deeper into the dark. The dark which is infectious, because one person's sins can lead others to sin, which in turn can lead others to do the same. This is how the dark has spread around the world to cover mankind with a shroud of sin which tries to hide and deny The Light.

Now is the time to reflect on how each one of us has allowed the dark to enter into our lives. Then in humility see, by God's grace, where we have gone wrong and ask The Lord to help each one of us to truly accept The Light within, The Light which will burn away our pride and help us to be the humble people we are meant to be. It is then through this humble love of God that The Divine Light is allowed, by our free will, to shine brightly in our lives. So that when we live, we live in The Light of Christ and let His Divine Light shine through us to touch others and bring them into His Light. This is the time to let the Light of Christ lift us out of the life that leads to death in sin so that we can truly live and be free in Him becoming the beacons of His love we are created to be.

He is risen now let us rise in The Divine Light of His love. In doing so let us remind Lucifer of his defeat, let us not fear the evil one and the darkness of his hatred and the hatred of those who serve him. Instead let us in the light of true love step forward bravely with complete trust in the glorious victory of Christ, The Lord, and show all the world what The Light brings into life—goodness, peace and love. Let us step out with The Light shining brightly through us burning away the corruption inflicted upon the world by the dark so that the pure love of God can reign in all lives. Let us stand up against the darkness of evil with the joy in our hearts of loving God and allow His joy through us destroy the misery the dark has brought into the world. By God's grace each person who loves Him can be a magnifier of The Divine Light shining His beautiful rays of love into the shadows of sin illuminating those dark areas and causing evil to flee back from whence it came. It is evil that fears The Light, mankind should not fear the dark but should know the dark has been overcome and should not be afraid to confront the dark ones, knowing that if they do so in Christ, The Lord, the evil ones in imitation of Lucifer will scream out in torment as they flee back into the recesses of hell.

TENDER LOVE

THE TENDERNESS THAT Jesus, Christ, The Lord, showed to all people is the same tenderness each of His followers are meant to show to others.

The gentle Master set before mankind the template on how to live in the true ways of God and that template is one shaped in love, in tenderness, in compassion, in gentleness, in forgiveness, in mercy, in service and in sacrifice.

Those who desire to follow Christ in true imitation of Him should make every effort to live to this template. If a person does not then they cannot really consider themself His follower as they do not follow His ways.

Many today have little tenderness towards others, instead so many look upon others with harsh eyes and with a demanding and condemning spirit. No one who truly loves Christ would be this way because they would know this is the wrong way to be. Those who love Christ would look upon others with a tenderness that imitates His tenderness. A tenderness that sees each person as a beautiful creation of love that needs nurturing in love so as to grow to be the person they were created to be.

With a tender heart and tender words a follower of Christ would reach out gently with loving encouragement and with understanding of the weaknesses of others. There would be no condemnation, no judgement, no feelings of superiority, only the desire to embrace others with the love of Christ and in His gentle love to bring each one to Him so that they can experience His merciful forgiveness and love. Even with those who may have hurt or taken advantage of a follower of Christ, the one who loves Christ would only respond with forgiveness and love, knowing this is what their divine Lord expects from them. The Lord, Jesus, showed all in His life on earth how to love. Unfortunately even many of His followers forget to follow His example and instead follow their own way which they often blend in with Christ's way, changing His way to be no longer that. Many prefer to put the way they believe love is to be lived and expressed before the way, The One Who is love, showed us. Because of this so many have a love that is a weak love as it is full of self and not full of God. With a love like this it becomes easy to turn away from those in need, to condemn those who do not live as the person thinks they should live, to reject the sinner instead of trying to help them and to put love of self before love of God and of others.

Some even give their love titles like "Tough love". True love is never tough it is always soft, tender and gentle while standing firmly in the truth.

True love does not accept sin or permit sin to happen but does not force the sinner with tough love to change. True love with tenderness offers the sinner the help and encouragement they need and where necessary places boundaries that the sinner should accept if they are to be helped, boundaries which of course prevent the sinner from drawing the person of true love into sin or into the acceptance of sin. Boundaries that would prevent the sinner from causing harm to others or to themselves.

Today some use what they call tough love and in fact are not showing the tenderness of true love but the hardness of heart that comes with a weak or false love and then in pride use the title of tough love to make themselves feel better about the way they are behaving.

It is often through what is called tough love that Christians do not reflect Christ but reflect the hardness of the world and in this hardness drive some away from God and not lead them to Him. It is through this tough love that often people are led to reject The Lord, Jesus, and not to embrace Him for they see in the followers of Christ who behave this way no difference from others in the world. The others who condemn the sinner, accuse the sinner and turn away from the sinner. They see no reason to reach out to Christ for help for they expect the same treatment from Him as they receive from His followers who are tough on them. It is easy now for a fear of God to grow and even the feelings that God does not or could not love them.

With these feelings on their hearts the sinner is opened more and more to evil's embrace of hatred and can so easily be led further away from God. The sinner who receives tough love so often does not see love at all but only the demands placed upon them by others and the condemnation of others, behaviour which is an imitation of some of the Pharisees in Holy Scripture. The Pharisees, who were quick to judge, quick to condemn and quick to punish.

However, The Lord, Jesus, showed clearly this was and is not the way of love. He showed the sinner, even as He died on the cross, a tender love that offered forgiveness, mercy and the way to redemption. His example of tender love is so easily forgotten by many, rejected in pride by many and replaced with a self centered way that has little love in it.

All who truly want to follow Christ, The Lord and truly want to imitate Him should have no hardness within them only softness. They should not have demanding hearts but tender ones that seek always to show the gentleness of Christ to all. They should not seek to force the sinner to change but in true imitation of Christ, through a compassionate and sacrificial love, encourage the sinner to see the error of their ways. Then in love take the sinner's hand softly so as to lead them to find fullness of life in the mercy of God which in itself will bring about the change needed.

Today so many who claim to love and follow Christ believe it is they who have to do everything and forget that Christ, The Lord, calls us to be true examples of His love through which He can work to bring about the necessary conversion of hearts. Each follower's role is one of a partnership in Christ, where the follower takes Christ's love out gently to all and then allows God to reach out through them to do the rest.

So many today do not allow God to play His part because they are too busy trying to fulfil that role themselves. Many forget it is through God's grace that people find salvation, grace that is poured out through those who in love serve God and fellow man. While each one who serves God has an important role to play each one should remember that God calls them to be living vessels of His love, vessels which allow His grace to flow through them so that lives can be changed as hearts and souls are converted. For this to happen each one has to put their will and their own expectations aside and bow humbly to the will of The Lord so that no barriers are placed between the grace of God and those who are meant to receive it.

It is always to be kept in mind that it is Christ, The Lord, who is the Master and His followers who are the servants, servants of love. It is in gentle and loving service people serve as God expects them to and it is with tender, sacrificial hearts people love as God expects them to. There is no place in the life of a true follower of Christ for hardness of heart or for coldness of spirit. Christ's Spirit is The Holy Spirit, the loving Spirit. The spirit all His followers should have. The spirit which is tender and merciful, that truly shows the love of God to all even in the most difficult of circumstances.

Hope

THE HOPE MANY have for a good future and a good life often excludes God and places all hope in the world and in the ways of man. With a hope like this then it is certain that truly life and the future will never achieve the goodness that is possible only in God, a goodness that is full and complete. The way of man and the way of the world can only ever bring a future that is empty of true meaning and true life.

Without God hope becomes filled with self and with earthly desires rather than heavenly and eternal desires. A hope that is centered on what the world can give and what man can create is a hope that is bound to lead into disaster for this kind of hope is the kind that opens people and the world to evil. A hope like this is filled with pitfalls that are there to draw people away from God and into hopelessness. A hope like this leads along the path of despair for in the end the world cannot give what a person truly needs and all the creations of mankind cannot satisfy the soul.

True hope is a hope that seeks to live in the goodness of God not only in this life but in eternity. Any other hope than that is a false hope that will in the end lead to disappointment and misery. Many, sadly, are deceived or deceive themselves into believing that their hopes can be answered in the world alone. The only hopes that can be answered in the world alone are self centered hopes which are ones that so often seek the best only of material things and ignore the spiritual needs and the needs of true love.

True hope is a hope that not only seeks good for self but good for all mankind seeing all as deserving of a future that is full of true love and a fulfilled life in God. With this seeking of good for all a person opens their heart in a true acceptance of the equality of all people and sees all as brothers and sisters who should be given respect and should be helped to have all that is needed in life.

This is the hope God has for mankind that they love Him and in His love they love one another equally. It is in this hope that God sent His only Son, The Lord, Jesus Christ, to show all how they are meant to live, to offer them the grace they need to live this way and to offer them all they need in life. The Lord also came to bring hope to those who had none, to those who despair and to those who were lost in life. He called out to all "I am your hope for a full life on earth and an eternal life of love in heaven".

The Lord, Jesus, also hoped that all people would listen to His words in Holy Scripture and come to live them in imitation of Him as they are supposed to.

To live in imitation of The Lord, Jesus, people should be hope-bringers just as The Lord is. To live as The Lord wants people to they should go out to all and lead all to the hope of a better life in Him. To live in imitation of The Lord, Jesus, people have to confront the despair that sin and evil bring with the hope that the love of God brings.

Every person on earth should be living a life of hope with the opportunity to have their good hopes fulfilled and all those in power, with influence and with wealth should be doing all they can to help the less well off have the opportunities they need and deserve to achieve this.

Mankind's true hopes can be found and brought to fruition in Jesus Christ, The Lord of hope, or can be lost and destroyed in self and in sin.

God hopes mankind will make the right decision while evil hopes mankind will make the wrong decision.

Each person needs to think carefully about which decision they will make and consider the cost of making the wrong one.

ADORATION OF THE LORD

To adore The Lord is an important part of loving God as in
adoration true love is evident and true love is strengthened. In the presence of The Body, Blood, Soul and Divinity of The Lord, Jesus, in The Blessed Sacrament the grace
of divine love fills the air and fills the people present even
if they do not feel or experience this. As God pours out
His grace to those who have come in true and humble love
before Him they are embraced by God and lifted on high
to join those in heaven perpetually adoring The Lord. In
the company of the angels and saints each one in adoration becomes part of the eternal chorus of love that sings
out the praises of God in divine worship. As part of that
chorus a person's soul resonates in love as it is touched
with the delights of heaven. That is why there are those at
adoration who have a burning desire within to give their
hearts to God. Why many feel like falling to their knees
and calling out their love for God and feel their hearts
aching within their bodies, aching with the desire to be
totally absorbed into God's holy presence; this truly is a
heavenly desire. While most of those who come to adoration may not experience this on the worldly planes of
the physical, mental and emotional, all experience it on
the spiritual and mystical levels even if this is unknown
to them. That is why so many who attend adoration find
a peace and a comfort that they cannot find elsewhere.
These feelings are results of the soul being touched by
God's grace in His presence. Some find answers coming
to them for the problems or questions in life that they
may have. This again comes from God's grace, which fills
the spirit with the knowledge and wisdom it needs. Others achieve a happiness just being in The Lord's presence,

this comes from the joy of soul as the soul is lifted to become part of the chorus of love with the heavenly citizens.

Every moment spent with The Lord in adoration is a moment where faith is strengthened and faith grows as in these moments the power of faith, which is the love of God, is revealed in its glory. This divine power, which is residing in the Blessed Sacrament, pours out to bless the faith of those present with gifts and graces that can and will lead not only them but those with whom they come in contact with to holiness. This happens when those who have come in adoration go out to the world with the peace and joy God has bestowed upon them and share it in all they do and with all they meet. This divine power also blesses every parish that has adoration for it not only is strengthening the faith of the parish but it also draws people together into a community of love centered on The Lord. This love brings individuals and families to unite as a true community of God that focuses on His divine presence and His divine love. Then through this community and through the ever present fullness of God in the Blessed Sacrament the divine power of God's loving presence pours out over the neighbourhood to flood it with blessings. This is why so often people say that since adoration began in their parish the whole area has changed for the better and that people who have been away from the church are returning.

This is a microcosm of what is happening worldwide as the power of the presence of the Lord in parishes around the world is poured out in an unseen light that illuminates the darkness all around. It is this presence of The Lord that is a bastion of heavenly grace which counters and defeats the action of evil on both the spiritual and the worldly levels. Sometimes the work of God's grace goes unnoticed as it is occurring beyond the human sight and perception in the realm of the spiritual. However, eventually the effect of God's grace in the spiritual becomes clear in the world as people's lives are changed because the evil around them, that has been attacking them in the spiritual realm, has been driven away and so peace returns to life and people are more open to God and to His will.

There is a simple divine truth and that is the more people will adore The Lord in true and humble love the more the world will be blessed and the more souls will be saved because of this. Today so few come and adore The Lord because so many have been blinded to this divine truth and so see little reason to spend time with The Lord. The people of God need to reflect on this truth and ask the Holy Spirit to help them see the true blessing of The Lord's Eucharistic presence and to help them spend time with The Lord. Then watch with The Lord as the world changes by the grace and power of God's presence amongst them.

Matthew 26:40 "So you could not keep watch with me for one hour?"

Messages Given By The Holy Spirit

ANGELS

6/5/04

THE ANGELS OF GOD are spirits sent to protect you from the spirit of evil.

ASK

2/2/98

ASK AND IT IS GIVEN but you must accept and believe to receive.

Jeremiah 51:14 | I will fill you.

BELIEF

6/5/98

IF YOU BELIEVE IN ME you will know security, peace and comfort. If you believe in Me you will know love, contentment and hope. If you believe in Me you will know truth, certainty and gentleness.
With belief in Me all good things are yours.

BLESSINGS

14/6/97

BLESS THE HEARTS of those who oppose you and in doing so
you bless your own heart by your humility.

13/5/05

WHEN MY GRACE IS ACCEPTED into a life then that life
becomes a grace-filled blessing for mankind.

CALLING ON THE SPIRIT

21/11/98

WHEN A PERSON calls on Me I answer.
When a person looks for Me I am there.
When a person seeks Me I am with them.
All it takes is for the person to make the decision and to
accept what I offer.
Isaiah 12:7 | they look.

15/8/00

WHEN A PERSON CALLS IN LOVE for My gifts and graces
I respond in love by giving them what is truly needed.

10/9/04

THOSE WHO WILL CALL ON ME in love will never be left
unanswered.

9/12/04

WHEN YOU CALL ON ME in love I respond in My grace-filled
love to gift you from My love.

CROSSES

14/8/98

EACH CROSS IS a grace,
Each cross is a gift,
Each cross is a sign of God's love for you.
Lamentations 3:22 | the favours of the Lord.

Embracing God

20/3/96

A PERSON WHO EMBRACES the work God gives them will be
rewarded over and over.

A person who embraces the love God offers them will be
filled and filled.

A person who embraces God's children as their family
will find eternal joy awaiting them.

27/6/06

EVEN THOUGH A person may be a sinner I am there for them
waiting to help them in any good way.

I wait hoping that each person, each sinner will turn and
ask for My help so that I can bring peace, joy and true
love into their lives.

I wait hoping that each person will embrace all that I
have for them and in that embrace find eternal life in
heaven with the Father and the Son and Me, the Holy
Spirit.

Every Day

15/1/98

EVERY DAY ASK OF ME and I will give.

Every day thank Me and I will be happy.

Every day receive for others and you will find I will give
you more as your humility will make me happy.

Ezekiel 37: 9 | come O spirit.

11/9/98

EACH DAY IS FILLED with My love, if you look you will see it.
Each day is filled with My gifts, if you look you will find
them. Each day is filled with God for each day is God's.

Psalm 103: 2 | Do not forget the gifts of God.

TURNING YOUR LIFE OVER to Me must be done daily.

EVERY DAY ASK FOR THE LIGHT of My love to illuminate your
 soul and it will.

EXAMPLES

BE AN ENCOURAGEMENT to others by the example of your life.
 1 Timothy 4:15 | *evident to everyone.*

FAITH

IN THE FAITHFUL you see the joy of loving Me.
 In the faithful you see the joy of loving each other.
 In the faithful you see the joy of God.
 Wisdom 18:1 | *Your holy ones had very great light.*

BE STRONG IN YOUR FAITH and you will be strong in My gifts.
 Mark 5:36 | *Just have faith.*

A SIMPLE FAITH is the best faith.
 Romans 16:19 | *good and simple.*

FAMILY

FAMILY LIFE CAN BE A GIFT of joyful love or it can be a burden
 of hate and anger.
 With God in a family joyful love runs supreme.
 Without God a family is not a true family and often slips
 into hateful anger that destroys those in and around it.

Fear

21/5/99

IF YOU LET FEAR into your heart you weaken the trust you
have in Me.

14/9/05

NEVER FEAR EVIL for if you live in the love of Jesus, evil
cannot harm you.

Foolishness

13/12/07

EVERYONE IS OFFERED GIFTS and graces by Me but not all
accept them. Some do not accept them because of
disbelief, some because of indifference and some because
of their pride. Then there are those who do accept that
which I offer but because of their selfishness do not
share them or because of their arrogance believe they are
better than others.
Sadly many people for various reasons deny My graces
and gifts or do not use them as they should and so
what I give shrivels and dies. The whole of mankind is
the worse for this as in denying Me and what I offer
mankind opens itself to the evil one and what he offers
and that is only pain and suffering. What foolishness!

27/6/06

ONLY THE BLIND, the foolish and the sinful deny Me.

Force

25/9/00

YOU CANNOT FORCE PEOPLE to love Me so do not try to.

Forgiveness

4/5/01

LET LOVING FORGIVENESS be in your heart always and you
will find My grace flowing through you.

FORGIVENESS IS THERE FOR ALL who will seek it in the spirit
of truth. Forgiveness is there for all who will seek it in
the spirit of mercy. Forgiveness is there for all who will
seek it in the spirit of love.
I am the Divine Spirit of love, who showers mercy upon
those who come truthfully seeking the Sacrament of
Confession, and truthfully open their hearts confessing
their sins.

Acts 9:31 | the holy spirit.

DO NOT LET YOUR SPIRIT become embittered because of
the difficulties others cause you. Instead, let your spirit
always be one of forgiveness and love for all no matter
what they do to you. It is in doing this your spirit
becomes one in My Holy Spirit.

FREEDOM

A BIRD CAN GLIDE freely on the wind that blows in the air.
A person can live freely on the wind that blows from My
Spirit.

Romans 9:1 | with the holy spirit.

GIFTS AND GRACES

GIFTS ARE GIVEN to many but often they do not or cannot
understand this because their mind refuses to accept
what it does not see. To use the gifts properly one must
accept them and then understand they are not only for
you but also for all your brothers and sisters. It is in the
accepting and the giving that the gifts come to fruition.

THE HEARTS OF MANKIND can be filled with the gifts and
graces of God if only they want to be. Mankind has only
to ask and then accept God's gifts to receive them.

IN THE GIFTS I GIVE to mankind is the key to true life. When
the gifts are seen for what they are and that is to give
to others and not for oneself, then the gifts grow as the
person begins to humble self in helping others and in
serving God. The charisms are there to heal not only
those to whom they are offered but also for those who
receive and share the gifts.

THE GIFTS I OFFER are gifts of love.
The graces I give are graces to save.
The light I shine is the light of God.
When the light of My love touches souls it brings My
gifts and graces which offer salvation to all, salvation
that is found in Jesus.

*1 Corinthians 2:5 | so that your faith should not depend on
human philosophy but on the power of God.*

THE GIFTS ARE THERE, use them.
The graces are there, share them.
The love is there as a gift to be shared, a gift that is full
of graces.

IN MY LOVE ARE THE GRACES and gifts that heal souls,
mend hearts and repair broken bodies. In My love are
the graces and gifts that bring the lost home to God.
In My love are the graces and gifts that show the mercy
of God.

MANY SEEK GIFTS and when they get them believe they are
theirs. Many seek gifts and when they receive them
only see their glory in them. Many seek gifts and when
they are given often do not believe or doubt in their
gifts.

When you ask for gifts believe you will receive them and
you will, but they will only stay if you share them and
use them for the glory of God.

*Job 37: 21 | There are times when the light vanishes behind
darkening clouds.*

Wisdom 13: 6 | For perhaps they go astray.

THE GIFTS OF LOVE, healing gifts of God.
The gifts of faith, the healing gifts of God.
The gifts of forgiveness, the healing gifts of God.
I offer these gifts to all and all should accept them.

THE GIFTS I give are given in love to be used and shared in love.
The gifts I give are for all.
The gifts I give are not a sign I love one person more
than another, they are a sign I love all people, for the
gifts are there for all people to share in love.

1 Timothy 6: 19 | So as to win the life that is true life.

THE GIFTS I HAVE are there for all.
The gifts I offer I offer to all.
The gifts I shower I shower upon all.
It just needs everyone to open their hearts in humble
love to receive them.

EACH PERSON IS given gifts to complete what I ask of them.
The gifts are given in different ways for different tasks

and the gifts are given in the way I will them to be. So
accept that and accept that others receive also.
Isaiah 53:10 | *the will of the Lord*

6/6/98

THE GIFTS I GIVE are for the betterment of all mankind, not
only for the needs of an individual. If you look you can
see this is true for all of My gifts.
1 Corinthians 10:24 | *No one should seek his own advantage.*

3/11/98

WHEN YOU ARE FILLED with My love you fill others with Me
But this is always by My grace.
Mark 12:11 | *By the Lord this has been done.*

10/7/99

ALL PEOPLE CAN BE FILLED with My gifts if they want to be
and if they seek them.
Sirach foreword | *living in conformity with the divine law.*

1/10/99

I GRACE EACH PERSON.
I gift each person.
I endow each person so that united in Me the graces and
gifts I endow mankind with will bring them to a strong
and true love of God. It is each person's choice to accept
or deny what I offer, to accept or deny God, to accept or
deny true life.
John 1:9 | *The true light.*

10/6/00

I BESTOW UPON THOSE who love Me graces and gifts to share
in love with others.
I bestow upon those who love Me the power to change
hearts and souls.
I bestow upon those who love Me the grace to take to
the world the truth of God and in that truth the power
to change the world for the better.

IT IS WITH LOVE I give My gifts and it should be with love
they are accepted, used and shared.

MY GIFTS, My graces, My glorious love—there for all people.
Those who will accept Me into their lives will find My
glorious love lifts each one of them high into My grace
and in My grace My gifts will fill their lives.

MY GRACE SURROUNDS YOU, My gifts fill you,
My love strengthens you.
All you who are baptized in Jesus' name and accept what
the Father offers you through Me, His Holy and Divine
Spirit.
*1 Corinthians 12: 13 | for in one spirit we were all baptized,
whether Jews or Greeks, slaves or free persons, and were all
given to drink of one spirit.*

THERE ARE GIFTS in all hearts but not all believe this.

ALL THOSE BAPTIZED in the Holy Trinity are baptized in the
fire of My love and are given the gifts and graces to see
them through life safely.
Sadly, some do not accept these gifts and graces and are
lost in life and the world.

MY GENTLE LOVE reaches out to all to fill them with grace.
All each person needs to do for My grace to fill them is
reach out in love and accept it.

MY GIFTS AND MY GRACES are available to all My people,
none are denied except those who deny themselves.

GRACE IS THERE for everyone and anyone who asks for it will receive the grace that is best for them.

EVERYONE WHO IS BAPTIZED in the Name of the Father, the Son and the Holy Spirit is offered My gifts and graces to make their lives and the lives of others good lives.

EVERY GRACE YOU RECEIVE is meant to be used for all people not just yourself.

TO SHARE MY GIFTS is essential if you want them to become stronger.

IN BAPTISM all are gifted and all are graced and all should believe this and seek to use what they have been given.

THE WHOLE WORLD needs My grace, even if this is not understood by most.

EACH PERSON'S SPIRIT can only reach its full potential in and by My grace.

WITH EVERY GIFT comes the responsibility to share it and to use it for the good of all.

GRACES AND GIFTS abound in the lives of those who love Me.

IN MY GRACE IS ALL a person needs to live a full life and this is a gift I offer to all.

MANY DO NOT UNDERSTAND My gifts and graces, as they see with human eyes and limitations. All should remember that I do as I will for the good of mankind, not as mankind wills as good for them.

9/7/07

MY GRACES AND GIFTS are for all people, not just for those through whom they flow.

25/8/07

EVERYONE CAN RECEIVE My gifts if they desire them and desire them not for themselves but for the good of others.

GIVING

19/6/99

WHEN YOU GIVE unceasingly for Me, I give unceasingly to you.

10/5/06

GIVE TO OTHERS as you expect Me to give to you; lovingly and abundantly.

27/6/06

TO TITHE give what you can afford without taking from your family's basic needs. That is all I expect, but sadly many in My name demand so much more; more which they usually use for their plans, not Mine.

GOD'S OFFERING

17/8/07

TO ALL PEOPLE I OFFER LOVE, graces and gifts.
   It is an offer all would be wise to accept, as in doing so they would accept all they need for a full and happy life on earth and beyond.

GOD'S WILL

27/3/96

IN TRUST IT HAPPENS...God's will.
   In doubt you block it...God's will.
   In life live it...God's will.

To do My will is to love Me, to serve Me and doing the
same for your brothers and sisters on earth.

In the centre of all you do must be My love if you want
to do My will.

Goodness

Goodness is all around but most are too blind to see it.

Goodness is what all should seek in their lives.
This is what all souls long for and all spirits can be set
free with, as it is in goodness all were created and all
were meant to live in, by, and for.

Happiness

Be happy in your work.
Be happy in your life.
Be happy in your God.
Colossians 1:8 | *in the spirit.*

Healing

A healthy mind, a healthy body, a healthy soul make a
healthy person. If but one of these is sick then a person
cannot be completely healthy.
For any sickness turn to Me and find I will heal your
soul which will ease your mind and comfort your body.
In Me find complete healing, find a holy healing and find
a fruitful and joyful life that comes with My love.
Revelations 2:10 | *I will give you the crown of life.*

MY GRACE CAN HEAL any problem and that is the gift I offer to all people.

IN MY LOVING TOUCH all who seek it can find complete healing of their life.

HEAVEN

THE SPIRITS OF THOSE who love Me will be lifted one day with their bodies into heaven through the love of Jesus with Whom I am One.

KEEP LOOKING HEAVENWARD to your final destination and never lose sight of your goal and the road you have to walk to get there.

HELPING OTHERS

PEOPLE NEED LOVE.
People need understanding.
People need help.
Offer help to all people to understand My love so that all their needs can be answered.
Isaiah 25: 8 | The Lord Yahweh will wipe away tears from every cheek

BE AWARE of the feelings of others and consider them always.
Philip 4: 2 | Understanding in the Lord.

DO NOT CONDEMN OTHERS for the wrong they do. Instead, in love guide them to do what is right.

IN EVERY PERSON encourage a spirit of true love by leading them from the false love promoted in the world and leading them to the true love existing in Me.

6/5/04

WITHIN EVERY HEART that truly loves is a door way for My grace to enter. Some people, however, need help in opening this door to Me. All those who know the love of God, should be there to help those who do not open this door.

10/4/05

IF YOU TRY TO HELP others in need because you love them, you do well.

12/3/07

WHOEVER TURNS TO ME IN LOVE will be rewarded with gifts and graces in abundance that they can share with others so as to help others turn to Me in love also.

HOLY

9/5/04

EVERY WORD spoken in love about holiness becomes holy in itself.

10/5/04

ALWAYS PRAISE THOSE who do holy work.

HOPE

14/9/98

WHEN YOU SEE OTHERS without hope bring them to Jesus so they can find it.
Mark 4:14 | *the sower sows the word.*

16/9/98

IT IS WITH HOPE IN ME in your heart that you will find your true path in life.
Ecclesiasticus 5:17 | *which God gives him.*

IN THE HOPE OF SUCCESS, in Me step forward and succeed.

HOPE FOR ALL PEOPLE to find My grace and pray for that to happen.

HUMILITY

HUMILITY IS FOUND in recognition of My Divinity and your humanity.

TO GROW IN GRACE a person needs to humble themselves before Me and before their fellow man.

HUMILITY MEANS to make yourself little before God and man in love and in service.

HUMOUR

YOUR WORDS MUST NEVER MOCK ANOTHER for in doing so you hurt them and you hurt yourself by the evil you let into your heart.

Jeremiah 51:24 | the evil.   Luke 1:64 | He spoke.

I AM

EVEN IN PLACES you least expect, I Am.

WHEN YOU THINK IT IS QUIET, I am at work.
When you think nothing is happening, I am at work.
When you think there is little being done, I am at work.
I am always at work, believe it.

Psalm 147:15 | The Lord sends a command to earth.

THE ONLY GHOST people should seek is Me, as *I am* the Holy
  Ghost.

IN THE SPIRIT

14/5/00

WHEN YOUR SPIRIT is in My Spirit and My Spirit is in yours,
  in that union all is possible in your life.

10/6/00

WHEN YOU LIVE in the spirit of love and caring you live in Me.

20/1/01

IF YOU HAVE A SPIRIT OF LOVE then you live in the right spirit.

27/11/07

IT IS ONLY in the Spirit of love you can do My will. I am the
  Spirit of love and it is in Me you will find the gifts and
  graces of love you need to fulfil your destiny.

6/5/04

EVEN THOUGH THE APOSTLES and Disciples had walked with
  Jesus and listened to His Holy Words, still they did not
  understand what He was saying until My grace came
  into them.
  Today it is the same, there are many claiming to walk
  with Jesus and to live to His Word but sadly they do not
  understand how to, as they live in the spirit of the world
  and not in the Spirit of God.

INSPIRED

31/10/96

INSPIRED TO DO God's work.
  Inspired to spread God's Word.
  Inspired to share God's love...those who love God.

I INSPIRE MANY PEOPLE and when you see those whom I
inspire, be grateful for the God-given gift they are.

JEALOUSY

16/5/04

DO NOT HARBOUR ANY JEALOUSY as in doing so you leave
the door open to evil.

JESUS

22/9/96

IN THE WOUNDS OF JESUS, hide your fears.
In the heart of Jesus, place your love.
In the Spirit of Jesus, find your strength.
In Jesus find all you need to live a life of love, a life without fear and filled with His strength to overcome evil.

22/11/96

MAKE YOUR HEART for Jesus.
Make your life for Jesus.
Make your work for Jesus.
Then make eternity yours with Jesus.
Isaiah 5:17 | then the lambs shall graze as in their pasture

13/10/96

WALK ON IN LOVE and succeed.
Walk on in faith and find the doors open.
Walk on in Jesus and see souls saved.
*Daniel 3:92 | Behold I see four men and walking in the
midst in the fire, and there is no hurt in them and the form
of the fourth is like the Son of God.*

31/1/97

IN THE HEART OF MAN is the heart of Jesus if only you believe
John 3:33 | anyone who believes in the Son

THE HEART OF JESUS is open to all waiting for them to come
to Him and ask.

He will always answer and answer in a way that only
brings goodness and hope into lives. Just ask and He
will answer.

Mark 2:5 | when Jesus saw the faith of these people.

THE PEACE YOU SEEK is only found in Jesus.

The strength you seek is only found in Jesus.

The love you seek is only found in Jesus.

Jesus' love will bring you the strength of heart to
remain peaceful no matter what happens.

Seek ye first Jesus' love for it is the kingdom of God and
you will find everything you need there.

*Matthew 6:33 | Seek first the kingdom of God and his
righteousness and all these things will be given you.*

TO ALL THOSE who will follow the way of the Son of God
I offer My gifts and graces so that they can bring His
glorious love alive in them and in others.

Psalm 106:47 | glory in praising.

Jeremiah 3:25 | The Lord.

MY PEACE IS UPON THOSE who love Jesus the Lord. My
power is with those who love Jesus the Lord. My gifts
are in those who love Jesus the Lord. Those who love
Jesus should take the power of My peaceful love to all
they meet by living in My peace and proclaiming My
peace to all in the name of Jesus, their Lord.

Jeremiah 44:20 | to all the people.

AS MY GRACE POURS OUT upon the world so pours out the opportunity for every person to be lifted to heights both spiritual and human that will bring them to the fullness of life and the fullness of love. Heights found only deep in the heart of Jesus, the highest of the high.
Titus 3: 15 | grace be with you all.

TO LIVE A HOLY LIFE do all you can to avoid sin and in all you do try to live as Jesus lived on earth.

JOY

IT IS WITH GREAT JOY I give My gifts to people, hoping that they will be received in joy and shared joyfully with others.

JUSTICE

IN MY LOVE JUSTICE REIGNS, a justice which may not be understood by mankind.
It is true justice which offers forgiveness for all who seek it with true repentance.

LEARNING

YOU WILL NEVER stop learning if you keep looking to Me with an open heart, mind and soul.

LIFE

IN LIFE there is a meaning,
In life there is a future,
In life there is a beginning.

Life is the beginning that can lead to a meaningful future.
Life with a meaning is the beginning of the future, for
life without a meaning can have no future, only an end.
The meaning of life is Jesus, the future of life is Jesus,
the beginning of life that never ends if Jesus, for Jesus
is life.

*1 Corinthians 2:9 | The things that no eye has seen and no
ear has heard, things beyond the mind of man, all that God
has prepared for those who love him.*

3/8/96

IN SPIRITUAL LIFE human life becomes complete.

Proverbs 11:22 | The blessing of the Lord, it maketh rich.

19/11/96

GLORIFY GOD in your life.

Praise God in your actions.

Thank God in your words.

Remember it is God who gives you life and acts through
your words and deeds to touch others.

*Matthew 21:16 | out of the mouths of infants and nursing
babies you have prepared praise for yourself*

3/3/97

A GIFT OF love...life.

A gift of life...love.

When you see life for what it truly is, God's gift of love,
then you truly treasure God's love in every life.

12/4/03

THE GIFT OF LIFE is given in grace and love and is to be
treasured in love.

24/2/04

MY GRACE IS WITH EVERY PERSON and My desire is that
every person accepts to live in My grace.

24/1/05

DO NOT KEEP YOUR FAITH in the Church, live it in the world.

MY GRACE is there for all so that all may live good, holy, and complete lives. Lives that will bring them home to heaven where they can live gracefully in eternity.

LIFE IS NEVER EMPTY for those who love Me as they know it is always full of My grace.

MY GRACE ABOUNDS in lives lived for God and reaches out through those lives to touch others, bringing them to live for God, then through their lives the cycle of grace is repeated.

SEEK TO LIVE A PURE LIFE by living the purest form of Catholicism which is in the Sacraments, in prayer, in Holy Scripture and in complete obedience to the Holy Catholic and Apostolic Church.

LOVE

IN GOD'S LOVE is all you need,
    In God's love is all.
    In God's mercy is all forgiveness,
    In God's mercy is all.
    In God's grace is all of mankind,
    In God's grace is all.
    God's merciful grace brings forgiveness to all if they
    turn in love and ask for it.

HOW IT HURTS when one you love abuses you. How it hurts when they turn their back on all the help you offer. How it hurts when you find it hard to trust them because of how they treat you.

72

How it hurts, but see that hurt comes from love, a love
that is still there, a love that will forgive if forgiveness is
asked for, a love that is a gift from God.

31/10/96

THE WAY OF LOVE is the way of God for when you truly love
you become a reflection of God's truth.

5/7/97

BREAKING BARRIERS, fixing hearts, saving souls...the love
of God.

23/7/97

THE LOVE IN YOUR HEART is shown by the love in your
words and actions.
The love in your heart is shown by the love in your giving
and caring for others.
The love in your heart is shown by your love of Me.

15/1/98

PREPARE YOURSELF IN LOVE, for without love how can you
expect to give love.
Prepare yourself in love, by accepting Jesus' love in the
Sacrament of the Eucharist.
Prepare yourself in love, by offering yourself to God in
service and love of others.

9/4/98

LOVE OVERCOMES PAIN.
Love overcomes hatred.
Love overcomes all.
Isaiah 8:7 | it shall rise above all

14/9/98

THINK OF MY LOVE ALWAYS and then you will be guided by
love in all you do...My love.
Psalm 103:11 | God's love towers over the faithful.

THE SPIRIT OF LOVE, the spirit of friendship, the spirit of caring is the spirit I want you to have.
2 Corinthians 6:6 | a holy spirit.

20/1/01

IT IS IN LOVE you will find your life becomes fulfilled; without love you will find your life empty.

15/12/02

THOSE WHO ASK in humble love of God for gifts and graces so that they can live in My love and share My love with the world will receive what they ask for.

27/9/03

NO ONE who loves Me truly would hate another.

18/5/04

THERE IS NO substitute for love.

19/3/05

IN LOVE UNITE with all those who love Me to spread My love.

6/4/06

ALL WHO SEEK MY GIFTS in love will receive them in love and be asked to share them in love.

15/4/06

WITH THE PASSION that you love Jesus, love all others.

17/8/07

I GIVE IN LOVE only expecting people to accept in true love.

10/10/07

IT IS THOSE who show true love of God who are truly open to My grace and My gifts as true love is the key that opens hearts and souls to Me.

MARRIAGE

15/10/96

THE LOVE FOUND IN A MARRIAGE is a gift from God that like all of God's gifts can grow if it is nurtured or can die if it is ignored. To nurture it, think of God's love in your life and in your wife's life and see your love united in God through your marriage.

Isaiah 12:5 | *Sing praise to the Lord for his glorious achievement.*

28/1/98

A MAN AND A WOMAN in marriage become one in love.
A man and a woman in marriage become one to God.
A man and a woman in marriage become inseparable in the eyes of God.
And when they keep love in their marriage they become inseparable in their own eyes also.

Matthew 6:10 | *on earth as in heaven.*

MARY

15/8/98

MARY WAS ASSUMED into heaven in an immaculate state.
Mary was assumed into heaven because of her immaculate life.
Mary was assumed into heaven the way she came into the world, immaculate.

Jeremiah 46:11 | *O virgin daughter.*

MISERY

28/11/98

A MISERABLE LIFE is a sinful life.
A miserable life is one without love.
A miserable life is the life those who live away from Me have, even though at times it may not seem so.
A miserable eternity awaits many of those unless they change their lives.

Ezekiel 31:14 | *those who go down into the pit.*

THE SADNESS OF A BROKEN HEART can be seen in the eyes of
those who are hurting in this way.
Numbers 24:16 | with eyes unveiled.

LIFE FOR THOSE WHO LOVE ME will be glorious in eternity
and for those who do not love Me it will be miserable
forever.

MONEY

DO NOT JUMP to the tune of money,
Dance to the tune of My love.

FOR MANY MONEY IS THEIR GOD while they reject the one
true God and foolishly worship that which will do
nothing for them in eternity except bring them suffering.

MOMENTS OF GRACE

EVERY MOMENT SPENT WITH, for, or thinking of God in love
is a moment of great grace.

OBEDIENCE

OBEDIENCE IS THE KEY to doing My will.
Obedience to God and obedience to the body of Jesus in
His Church.
Psalm 81:9 | if only you will obey me.

TO BE HOLY means to be obedient to God and obedient to
His Body on earth.
Titus 3:1 | to be obedient, to be open to every good.

Peace

27/6/98

PEACE IN YOUR WORDS,
    Peace in your hearts,
    Peace in your life is a gift I offer to all.
    Titus 1: 4 | peace from God.

5/7/04

WHEN THE WORLD accepts God's love as its way and rejects
    the ways of evil then peace will reign supreme.

Pentecost

18/5/02

MAKE EVERY DAY your Pentecost and stay on fire in My love.

8/6/02

ON THIS DAY the Church was set on fire with My graces and
    gifts.
    Today the same can happen in the lives of those who will
    come truly seeking those graces and gifts.

30/5/04 (Pentecost)

THE EYES WERE OPENED, the souls set on fire and the spirits
    empowered with My gifts and graces on this day of
    Pentecost.
    Every day can be a Pentecost for those who truly seek to
    see the truth and are prepared to take the flame of My
    love to all they meet.

Prayer

23/4/96

PRAYERS FOR OTHERS are also prayers that strengthen you,
    For when you give you receive.
    Ecclesiasticus 13: 26 | the mark of a good heart.

PRAYER, A POWERFUL WEAPON against evil.
  Prayer, a powerful gift from God.
  Prayer, an answer to the problems in the world.
  Isaiah 49: 4 | And all the while my cause was with Yahweh.

18/4/97

TO EMBARK on a journey of love pray to be filled with and
  guided by love.
  John 12: 26 | Let him follow me.

22/11/97

TO PRAY FOR THE WELL BEING OF OTHERS is a duty of all
  Christians for it is by loving others and wanting the best
  for them that you show you truly love.

16/4/98

IN PRAYER you will find your heart filled with My love, My
  gifts and My graces if you pray seeking to love Me more
  and to live in My love.

9/1/99

REACH OUT from your spirit in prayer and find your spirit
  touched by Me.
  Psalm 32: 18 | the spirit within.

27/2/99

IT IS EASY to be drawn into thoughts you do not want to
  have when you let your prayer life slip.
  Centre each day on the Eucharist and prayer then find it
  will be easier to keep from those thoughts and easier to
  love others instead of condemning them.

23/5/99 (Pentecost)

IF PEOPLE PRAY IN TRUTH and in love for My gifts and
  graces, how can I not answer their prayers, for I am
  truth and I am love. If people pray for their hearts to
  be opened more and more to Me, how can I not answer
  their prayers, for I long to fill hearts.

If people pray that their lives become complete in Me and that their lives are set alight in My love, how can I not answer their prayers, for I am the flame of love that brings lives into the true light and fills them with the gifts and graces of God.

1 John 4: 2 | this is how you can know the spirit of God.

21/8/99

PRAY FOR MY LOVE to set fire to the souls of others and your prayers will be answered.

Isaiah 66: 15 | The Lord shall come in fire.

19/2/00

THE POWER OF PRAYER is beyond mankind's understanding, for it is the power of God wrapped in the love and trust of the one who prays.

22/7/00

PRAYER IN THE SPIRIT OF LOVE is prayer that will open your soul to My Divine power.

Luke 24: 49 | power from on high.

3/7/04

WHEN A PERSON makes the effort to pray those prayers are listened to.

PRIDE

6/12/97

PRIDE CAN CLOUD ANYONE'S HEART if they are not careful and do not look to Me in all they do.

Sirach 2: 17 | ...and humble themselves before him.

16/4/98

WHEN YOU BELIEVE you have mastered one gift you will find you have only allowed your pride to tell you this and that the gift will get weaker instead of stronger.

Psalm 31: 24 | The Lord protects the loyal but repays the arrogant in full

YOUR SPIRIT CAN SHINE in My love or it can become dull in your pride.

YOUR PRIDE will always be with you but so will be the power to overcome it.

PRIESTS

A PRIEST can be a reflection of Jesus on earth by living a prayerful and sacramental life. When a priest lives a life full of the things of earth all he becomes is a reflection of society.

A PRIEST IS gifted.
A priest is graced.
A priest is loved.
And if they believe this then by My grace they can become a gift of love to all.
Psalm 25: 12 | God shows them the way.

IN THE CHURCH are many holy people.
In the church are many gifted people.
In the church are many serving people.
The people who are the priests.
Isaiah 66: 21 | some of these I will take as priests

HOLY WORDS, holy prayers, holy gifts, the words of a priest.
1 Corinthians 8: 40 | have the spirit of God

NEVER DENY A PRIEST RESPECT for the holy work they do.

PROMISES

19/6/99

ANY PRAYER to Me in love is answered.
   Anyone who calls on Me is heard.
   Any soul that is willing to love Me is filled with My Spirit.
   This is My promise and it is true.
   Psalm 19: 8 | *the decree of the Lord is trustworthy.*

RELYING ON GOD

2/8/97

MEN MAY FAIL when they rely on themselves but succeed
   when they rely on God.

RESPECT OTHERS

3/7/04

BE POLITE TO OTHERS at all times.

SACRIFICES

8/6/97

SACRIFICES ARE DIFFICULT otherwise they would not be
   sacrifices.
   Sacrifices can be graces if you accept them in love.
   Sacrifices can help you grow when you offer them to Me
   without bitterness and resentment.
   Proverbs 8: 15 | *and obtains the favour of Yahweh.*

23/4/06

IT IS GOOD to be prepared to sacrifice, as all who love God
   will be called to do so in one way or another.

SAFE

19/5/98

WHEN YOU PUT GOD FIRST you find you put yourself into
   His hands and are safe forever.

BE SECURE in My grace.
> Be safe in My love.
> Be sure in My power that gracefully surrounds you with
> My love to keep you safe and secure.

SEARCHING FOR GOD

WHEN PEOPLE COME in search of Me I give them every help
in finding Me.
> When people come in search of Me I give them every
> hope for the future.
> When people come in search of Me I give them every
> opportunity to be filled with Me and I do this for every
> person because I love them all.
> *Psalm 107: 6/7 | they cried to the Lord who rescued them
> in their peril, guided them by a direct path.*

SENT OUT

TO THE WORLD all those who love Me are sent but sadly only
a few go, most keep Me to themselves.

SERVANTS OF GOD

A TRUE SERVANT OF GOD LOVES.
> A true servant of God gives.
> A true servant of God is humble.

A SERVANT OF MINE serves others by serving Me as the
service I ask for is to bring My love to others.
> *Hebrews 12: 6 | Whom the Lord loves.*

MY POWER is the power of love.

My fire is the fire of love.

My servants must be servants of love if they want to serve Me, for the moment they step out of love they only serve themselves.

Isaiah 66: 3 | since they have chosen their own ways.

MY WORDS set fire to souls.

My gifts bring healing to lives.

My love touches and mends broken hearts.

And I do it through those who love and serve Me.

Leviticus 25: 42 | servants of mine.

MY POWER FLOWS through humble servants in great ways... be humble.

THE SPIRIT of a servant of Mine must be humble, for it is through humility My gifts become more powerful and bring My glory into the hearts of others.

MY GRACES, MY GIFTS, my love freely flow through those who trust in Me and who serve Me in humility.

WHEN A PERSON gives their life in service to Me, I give them all they need to complete that service.

MY GRACE CAN fill any person if only they truly seek it in humble love and humble service of God.

MY GRACE ABOUNDS IN THE LIVES of those who humbly serve Me.

My power, My love and My grace is seen in all those who truly love and serve Me.

5/2/07

Those who serve Me in love will be rewarded in heaven with eternal love.

Sharing Love

13/9/97

Gifted in love means to be gifted in giving for God and gifted in service to God by sharing His love with all.

25/9/97

The love of God in your heart becomes the love of God to others when you share it with them for the glory of God.

26/1/98

The love you share must be shared with all and without conditions.
The love you share must be seen as a gift that is given to you to give to others.
The love you share must be a love that is recognized as a grace that God gives to you.

27/1/98

There is a way of sharing My love that touches all.
It is called humble giving.

3/6/01

It is the grace I give to those who love me; the grace to share My love.

2/1/08

To use your gifts wisely share them in love with those in need and do not keep the gifts to yourself or use them only when you want.

THERE ARE MANY EMPTY LIVES waiting to be filled by Jesus and those who are already full of Him need to go and share this fullness with others.

SIN

8/11/96

TO SEE YOUR SINS is the first step to overcoming them.

17/1/98

THOSE WHO LIVE IN SIN will be destroyed by sin. Those who live in love will be saved by love. The choice is obvious, the choice is Jesus, for He is love.
Lamentations 4: 16 | *The Lord himself.*

1/9/00

TURNING YOUR LIFE from sin to sanctity is only possible in My grace.
John 16: 13 | *the spirit of truth, he will guide you to all truth.*

2/10/00

EVIL SPIRITS surround so many today because people live in an acceptance of sin and in so doing invite the evil ones to them.

24/12/03

NO SIN should ever be seen as acceptable.

24/12/03

DO NOT LET the fire of your spirit be smothered by the sins of others.

15/12/04

THE BATTLE WITH EVIL is to sin or not to sin.

9/2/05

TRY TO AVOID conversations that lead you towards sin.

LEGAL ARGUMENTS and legal manoeuvres do not and cannot
make sin acceptable or justifiable.

DO NOT LET THE WRONGS others do to you lead you into bad
thoughts. Always try to keep your thoughts good and holy.

SPEAKING WITH LOVE

9/5/01

WORDS FILLED WITH MY LOVE touch hearts regardless of
the language in which they are spoken.

SUFFERING

22/8/97

SOMETIMES PEOPLE SUFFER as a grace that helps to save
souls. Sometimes people suffer but suffer in joy as I fill
them with My love. Sometimes people suffer because
this is what I ask of them.
These people are graced in a way that helps them to love
Me more through the suffering they willingly carry for Me.

18/5/04

IF YOU SUFFER in doing My holy work, know many graces
are being granted because of this suffering.

THE CHOICE IS YOURS

12/3/07

IN EACH PERSON can be the spirit of good or of evil. It is up
to each person to decide which they want.

THE CHURCH

18/2/02

IN THE WORD OF GOD resides all the gifts and graces
mankind needs to attain holiness. In the Catholic

Church those gifts and graces can be seen in their
fullness.

8/6/02

BY MY GRACE, with My gifts, and in My love, the Church
grew and grew.
Today this can continue if like the early Church the
people say yes to My will.

4/6/06

THE CHURCH WILL NOT FALL even though at times it might
seem as if it will.
The Church is full of My grace and that grace cannot be
overcome and all those who believe in this will never be
overcome, either.

THE DEFEATED

15/4/06

SATAN IS ANGRY in his defeat, bitter in his downfall and
vengeful in his despair. So he stalks the world venting
his anger foolishly on the world hoping he may change
what cannot be changed and trying to hurt as many as
possible so as to hurt God.

THE EUCHARIST

18/5/02

IN THE WHOLE WORLD there is a vacuum of love that sin and
evil has created.
This vacuum needs to be filled with the Eucharistic love
and power of Jesus so that mankind can find true peace
in the heart of God.

15/5/05 (Pentecost)

MY GRACE FILLS ALL THOSE who are filled with Jesus in
the Eucharist when they receive Him with an open and
loving heart.

IT IS IN THE HOLY MASS your spirit can be made holy by the
presence of Jesus Who will fill you with holy grace.

25/8/07

PREPARE FOR THE EUCHARIST by thinking of the love
Jesus has for you when He comes into you lifting your
humanity into His Divinity.

THE FIRE OF LOVE

4/2/98

ON FIRE WITH MY LOVE anything is possible.
On fire with My love anyone can be touched.
On fire with My love any heart can be touched and it is
possible to light any soul with My graces.
Zepheniah 1:2 | *all things.*
Jeremiah 20:15 | *filling him with great joy.*

10/7/99

WHEN THE FIRE of My love touches hearts it changes them
into furnaces of love that will burn brightly and bring
My fire to others. The hearts only need to accept My love
and say yes to My will.
1 Maccabees 10:24 | *so that they may be an aid to me.*

13/10/99

IN EACH SOUL is a fire waiting to be set alight in My love.

20/1/01

IF A PERSON IS ON FIRE in My love they should be feeling
love for all people, if not then the love they feel for Me is
being smothered by their pride.
Hosea 1:2 | *turning away from the Lord.*

3/6/01

THE FIRE OF MY LOVE can touch every heart and it will
when those who love Me take My fire to all they meet.

As I pour out My fire upon the earth evil tries to smother
it with a blanket of sin but My fire will burn that blanket
away and bring My light to the world.
Psalm 102: 4 | Burn away as in a furnace.

In the heart of one who loves Me is a fire that burns so
brightly it can be seen throughout eternity.

When a person's spirit is on fire with love for Me they can
burn a bright path of love through the darkness of sin.

My fire will burn with love in any heart that will open
itself to Me.

The fire of My love brings peace into hearts, not turmoil.
When turmoil comes, it comes from the fires of hell.

The fire of love that burns in your soul burns brighter
every time you go to the Sacraments.

The fire of My love blazes in every heart that is open
to Me in humble love of God and not closed to Me in
prideful love of self.

The Gifted

Given gifts you must share them so that they may grow.
Given graces you must offer them for the good of others
so that you may receive more.
Given love you must bring it to others so it may be
strengthened.

THE GIFTED are only truly gifted when they share what God has given them.

THE GIFTED must share their gifts for them to grow.
The gifted must share their gifts for them to be strengthened.
The gifted must share their gifts for them to find more.
Isaiah 32:15 | *a spirit from high is poured out on us.*

THE GIFTED ARE ALL THOSE baptized in Jesus, but sadly some do not use or do not believe in the gifts they have been given.
Ephesians 4:7 | *Grace was given to each.*

TO THE GIFTED I SAY share your gifts as that is what the gifts are for.
Romans 8:1 | *the law of the spirit of life in Christ Jesus.*

THE GIFTED SHOULD SHARE THEIR GIFTS if they want them to grow.

WHEN PEOPLE SAY you are a gift, remember it is My gift in you that they are seeing.

ALL PEOPLE ARE GIFTED but not all accept and use their gifts and so mankind is denied many graces to help it reach its full potential.
John 4:10 | *the gift of God.*

A TRULY GRACED and gifted person always thanks Me for what they have.

WHEN YOU GIVE THANKS with a true heart for every gift, you show you are worthy to receive them.

24/3/06

ANY PERSON WHO WILL LOVE ME will be truly gifted by Me.

THE HEART

5/6/97

AN OPEN HEART and a truthful heart touches many.

22/11/97

A FLAME OF LOVE is in each person's heart. For it to burn brightly you just need to ask of Me and I will fan the fire with My gifts and graces.

Jeremiah 51:11 | *The Lord has stirred up the spirit.*

15/2/98

PRECIOUS HEARTS, precious souls, precious loves... The hearts of mankind whose souls I love and are precious to Me.

20/2/98

YOUR HEART must show love to all.
Your heart must deny none.
Your heart will then reflect Jesus' heart

7/4/98

IN MY HEART I love all people. How I wish all people returned My love and in their hearts loved me.

Ephesians 5:19 | *singing and playing to the lord in your hearts*

10/9/98

ALL HEARTS THAT ARE OPEN TO ME will be filled with My gifts and graces.
To open your heart to Me you need to close your heart to sin.

Psalm 51:12 | *a clean heart.*

91

WITH AN OPEN HEART to Me people can be filled with all
they need in their lives.
With a closed heart they can only live in need.
Titus 3:13 | *everything they need.*

WHEN THE HEART RULES THE HEAD it is a good thing for
then it is love that is reigning and as I am love it is I that
is guiding the mind.

WITH GENTLE WORDS hard hearts can be moved.

WITH A HEART OF LOVE your eyes only see with love.

A GOOD HEART is a loving, forgiving and sacrificing heart,
for it shows the heart of Jesus.

WHEN YOUR HEART IS OPEN TO ME your spirit jumps for joy
within as it is touched by My divine grace poured into
your heart.

THE HOLY TRINITY

WHEN YOU WELCOME ME in your hearts you welcome the
love of God, the light of God...God.
When you welcome me in your hearts you welcome the
Father and the Son, for though we are three, we are...One.

I WORK IN HEARTS to open them to My love and to accept
the truth of Jesus.
I work in hearts to heal them and remove all doubts so
they will believe in Jesus.
I work in hearts to bring eternal life to all in Jesus.

When I work it is with Jesus and the Father and anyone
who does not believe this does not accept the truth.
Psalm 55:22 | *War is in their hearts.*

28/4/99

WHEN THE TRUTH IS SPOKEN it lifts hearts and fills them
with the joy of knowing the truth—the truth which is
the divine Trinitarian nature of God.

17/6/00

IN THE FATHER and in Jesus I Am, just as in Me They are
and together We are One.
Daniel 2:27 | *the mystery.*

19/12/07

IN UNION with The Father and The Son I am The Holy Spirit.
God who is three yet one.

6/5/04

HOLY PEOPLE BECOME HOLY by their love of the Father and
the Son and Me in the Holy Trinity.

6/6/04 (Trinity Sunday)

IT IS A MYSTERY no one on earth can understand, the
mystery of the Holy Trinity, the One true God, but a
mystery that all can believe in if they choose to.

4/3/05

BY MY GRACE souls are drawn closer to Me as they are
opened to Me by the love of Jesus and by the desire of
the Father.

3/6/07

ONE HEART OF LOVE,
    One Who is love,
    One Spirit of love...
    The Holy Trinity.

THE LIGHT

15/1/98

WITH THE LIGHT in your heart, the darkness cannot take you.
Ask each day to have the light of My love and the fire of
My Spirit within you.

Jeremiah 21:14 | *I will kindle the fire.*

18/7/98

IN THE LIGHT OF LOVE sin flees.
In the light of love peace reigns.
In the light of love you will find peace waiting and sin
fleeing.
I am that light, the light of God.

Isaiah 59:10 | *Look for light.*

5/12/01

MY LIGHT, MY LOVE, and My grace pour out over the world.
All people need to do is accept these into their lives and
they will be happy.

THE PATH

30/1/99

SOMETIMES WHAT MAY SEEM like a difficult path to take
is the best path and in the long run the easiest so never
be afraid to make the difficult decisions as long as you
do so in love for the right reasons and in obedience to
the commandments.

THE POWER OF GOD

12/10/96

THE POWER OF LOVE,
The power of God.

The grace of love,
The grace of God.

The gift of love,
The gift of God.

God is love and all gifts and graces come from God's
power, which is love.

17/10/96

THE POWER OF GOD is the power of love so when you live
in My love you are filled with God's power which is love
itself.

17/1/98

THE POWER OF MY LOVE is in your heart and you can set it
free in humility.
Psalm 79:11 | great power.

27/3/99

THROUGHOUT HISTORY My power has been displayed in the
weak. Today it is the same.

11/12/99

IN MY POWER all is possible, for it is the power of God's love.
Sirach 43:12 | the mighty hand of God.

1/5/01

MY POWER is above all.
My power can overcome all.
My power can heal all.
Believe in My power for if you do all can be overcome
and any sickness can be healed because nothing is above
My power and all things are subject to it.

15/9/01

MY POWER IS LOVE so if you live in My love you will be filled
with My power.
My power is love and My love is all powerful for it is
Divine.

7/11/02

IN THE LEAST LIKELY MOMENTS My power can surprise you.

THE POWER OF MY LOVE is available to all who will love Me.

THE POWER OF MY LOVE is above all other powers and
    cannot be defeated by any other power.

THE ROSARY

30/11/96

THE ROSARY, a gift to bring mankind closer to God.
    The rosary, a sharing of God's love with mankind.
    The rosary, a grace through The Mother of God to bring
    the truth of God into mankind's hearts.
    Matthew 6:5 | when you pray

THE SACRAMENTS

4/6/98

TO TAKE MY LOVE TO OTHERS you must be filled with My
    love first and it is through the Sacraments you will be
    filled.
    Zepheniah 1:7 | in the presence of the Lord.

3/10/98

MY FIRE IS IN YOUR SOUL, feed it in the Sacraments.
    Luke 1:41 | filled with the Holy Spirit.

9/1/99

WHEN YOUR SOUL is laid bare before you in the Sacraments
    it hurts to see what is offensive to God, for if you love
    God then it is offensive to you, also.
    Malachi 1:5 | your own eyes shall see it.

19/8/00

SPIRITUAL GROWTH can be very strong and very deep by
    immersing your spirit in the Sacraments.

19/6/02

MY GIFTS AND MY GRACES come in the Sacraments.

A SOUL CLEANSED in the Sacrament of Confession is a soul
open to My grace.

2/10/02

YOUR SPIRIT can be open to My Spirit through the Sacraments.
Luke 4:18 | The spirit of the Lord.

12/4/03

SEEK HOLINESS through the sacramental life and you will
find it.

23/1/08

LET YOUR SPIRIT shine by being filled with My Spirit of light
in the Holy Sacraments.

27/11/07

YOUR SPIRITUAL NEEDS can be fulfilled in the Sacraments.

24/12/03

IT IS IN THE SACRAMENTS that true life, true faith and true
healing can be found.

12/3/07

THE TRUTH

WHEN YOU ASK IN TRUTH and in love for My glory then I
answer in love and fill you with the truth.
Proverbs 2:2 | inclining your heart to understanding.

21/1/98

THE TRUTH IS OFTEN MOCKED but still it remains the truth.

8/11/01

NEVER NEGOTIATE WITH EVIL, always stand firm against it
in My truth.

23/11/04

AS A PERSON ASKS OF ME in truthful love their soul is open
to receive the gifts and graces I desire to give to them for
the betterment of themselves and of all mankind.

23/2/06

THE TRUTH OF ALL LIFE

2/10/02

WHETHER OR NOT life exists on other planets is not the
answer on how life came to be or how it continues to be.
Life came from the Father through the Lord Jesus and
by the power of Me, the Holy Spirit.
Life continues to exist in the Lord Jesus by the will of
the Father and by the grace of Me, the Holy Spirit.
This is the truth of all life.

2 Chronicles 18:15 | the truth in the name of the Lord.

12/4/03

MY GRACE IS EVERYWHERE and everyone and everything
exists in it and of it.

Psalm 139:7 | where can I hide from your spirit?
From your presence where can I flee?

THE WAYS

20/7/96

THE SACRAMENTS, prayer and humility—the ways to grow
in truth and love.

THE WORD OF GOD

31/7/96

THE WORD OF God fills your entire being with love when
you accept it within.

Proverbs 16:24 | Kindly words are a honeycomb, sweet to
the taste, wholesome to the body.

4/2/98

THE POWER OF THE WORD is stronger than any sword for
the Word is Jesus.

Sirach 40:17 | goodness will never be cut off.

THE POWER OF THE WORD, the power of The Spirit, the
power of God.

PRECIOUS WORDS; HOLY Scripture.
Loving words; Holy Scripture.
God's Word; Holy Scripture.
Psalm 16:11 | *you will teach me the path of life.*

THE WORD OF GOD is love.
Psalm 22:9 | *He loves you.*

READING HOLY SCRIPTURE without living to its Holy Word
is like reading a manual for a machine but never turning
the machine on.

THE YOUNG

IN THE YOUNG is the future of mankind. Place God in their
hearts and the future is with God. Place sin in their
hearts and there is no future.
Hosea 8:6 | *destined for the flames*

IN CHILDREN SEE LOVE,
In children see joy,
In children see how you should be.
Psalm 8:3 | *Out of the mouths of babes and sucklings.*

TRUE STRENGTH

WHEN YOUR SPIRIT is filled with My love it is strong.
When your spirit is filled with self and pride it is weak.
When your spirit is filled with the longing to serve

me, the strength it will have is beyond human understanding.

Mark 2:12 | *we have never seen anything like this.*

True Wealth

8/11/98

THE WEALTH you must seek is the love I have for you.

John 16:24 | *that your joy may be complete.*

Trust

9/10/96

TRUST BRINGS THE GIFTS YOU NEED to do My work.
Trust brings all you need to live.
Trust brings your heart closer to Mine.

Wisdom 3:1 | *The souls of the just are in the hand of God.*

26/2/97

TRUST IS A virtue.
Trust is a grace.
Trust is a necessity for without trust what is there?

Psalm 37:5 | *commit your way to the Lord,*
trust that God will act.

2/3/97

TRUST IN ME brings rewards, rewards to share and in the
sharing trusting that more rewards will come.

10/4/97

IF YOU TRUST IN ME and if you commit yourself to Me then
all is possible.

Ezekiel 28:22 | *I will show my glory through you.*

14/6/97

PUTTING YOUR TRUST IN ME brings rewards you could never
have imagined.

2 Corinthians 9:6 | *Anyone who sows generously will reap*
generously as well.

TRUST IS THE KEY to working for Me, for without trust little
is possible.

Ecclesiasticus 7: 8 | *Better is the patient spirit.*

TRUST IN ME is very important; without such trust you
cannot succeed.

With it you cannot fail.

Luke 18: 7 | *will not God then secure the rights of the
chosen ones.*

IN TRUST you will achieve much.

In doubt you will achieve little.

Sirach 2: 13 | *woe to the faint of heart who trust not.*

UNDERSTANDING OTHERS

UNDERSTAND THE NEEDS OF OTHERS may seem different to
yours but in truth they are the same; all need the love
of God.

WAR

WHOEVER SEEMS TO WIN A WAR, in truth both sides lose.

IN WAR, MANY SIN and many are blinded to sin and make
excuses for it.

However, it should be remembered all have to answer for
sin and there is no reason that justifies sin.

THE SPIRIT OF WAR is evil not holy.

Weaknesses

22/2/97

SHORT OF TEMPER means short of love.

31/7/97

IF ALL PEOPLE recognized their weaknesses and came to Me
for strength the world would soon change to be a world
of humble love.
Sirach 23: 27 | And all who inhabit the world understand.
Isaiah 59: 8 | The way of peace.

3/4/98

IT IS WHEN YOU LOOK at yourself and see how your
weaknesses and failings affect your life, then see how
even with these you can still do goodness in your life,
that you start to come to terms with your humanity.
Isaiah 60: 5 | then you shall be radiant at what you see

19/11/07

MY GRACE POURS OUT POWERFULLY through the weakness
of those who humbly serve Me in love and so in Me their
weakness can become their strength.

Wisdom

20/1/01

THE WISEST THING to do in life is to live as Jesus asks you to.

8/11/02

IT IS A WISE MAN who does not worry, for worry changes
nothing.

5/2/05

A WISE PERSON is one who considers the needs of others and
not just the needs of self.

8/8/07

TRUE WISDOM IS A GIFT that all should seek through prayer.

Working For God

IN MY WORK find love,
   In My work find peace,
   In My work find hope,
   In God's work find everything.
   Matthew 9:57 | The harvest is abundant but the workers are only a few.

Worry

WHEN YOU DO NOT WORRY, you grow.
   When you do not worry, you are strengthened.
   When you do not worry, you show your trust in Me.
   Luke 24:38 | Why are you troubled?

LET YOUR WORRIES FALL FROM YOU like dead leaves fall
   from a tree leaving it ready to flower again with beauty.
   1 Timothy 2:15 | persevere in faith and love and holiness.

IF YOU WORRY OVER LITTLE PROBLEMS bigger ones may
   destroy you.

Letters

Paedophilia

TODAY, SADLY THE SCANDAL of evil paedophilia is raising its ugly head within the Catholic Church. A number of priests have been found guilty of this heinous crime against children and this offense against the moral laws of God. It is right and justifiable that people within and outside the church stand up and condemn these terrible acts so that those who have committed them can be brought to justice. It is also right to look at the processes that have allowed this to happen and to continue happening. Obviously there has been some lack of understanding in how to deal with these situations as they have occurred. We must pray that lessons have been learned from the past so that in future the correct actions are taken when facing this evil.

We as church must also face up to the responsibility we have in caring for those innocents who have been hurt and do our best to help them through any difficulties they may have because of what they had to endure. We also now have to stand united against this evil which has entered the church, for surely this is an attack of evil whose aim is to damage and break the church. The perception now is that many priests are immoral and evil when in fact the vast majority are good and holy priests seeking to serve God and fellow man. It is in fact a very, very small minority of priests who sin in such a way, yet, through the media, it appears as if this is commonplace among priests.

At present evil is launching a large attack on the good priests through the very few it has ensnared with sexual desires and deviations. Now is the time for all Catholics to support strongly and publicly their priests and not be drawn into the almost hysterical responses to what has happened. We must understand that in normal society a percentage of people behave in this terrible way but that does not mean all do. Priests are taken from society and so it is to be expected that a small percentage of them will have this sickness of evil within them but that does not mean all do. It does mean however that those seeking the priesthood must be scrutinized to a much greater degree than in the past, so that those with problems can be removed. We should realize too that these sick people in society will be drawn to vocations where children are placed in their care so that they can exploit this position. It does not only happen in the priesthood.

Today Catholics must be courageous in facing this threat to the church, not only courageous in helping root out this evil but also courageous in standing by their priests and proclaiming to the world that God in His love and mercy is working strongly in and through the priesthood. We must not let those who oppose the church use this time to push their own agendas, i.e. married priests, women priests, homosexual priests, to name a few. Instead, we must be firm in our faith knowing that God will, with our cooperation correct any wrongs in the church and will, through the church, bring His divine love to all.

We must not forget or ignore what has happened but we must forgive and we must stand with and in Christ to confront this evil which attacks His church today.

Let Bad Examples Now Become Good Ones

In LIFE TODAY so many walk away from the one true God, many who were brought up as Christian embrace the world instead of embracing Christ. While others who were brought up as Christian, but with little example of Christ before them in the lives of those around, turn to other religions that seem to give a clear spiritual and moral code by which to live.

Often those who remain Christian are quick to condemn and judge such people forgetting that the reasons many of these behave in such a way is because of the bad examples of faith some of those in the Church have been.

In the past and still today Church members have embraced the worldly ways over the ways of Christ.

Church members have remained silent as great wrongs such as homosexuality, adultery and divorce, promiscuity, the death penalty, war, contraception and abortion are promoted in the world as being right and because of this silence these great wrongs have been allowed to infect society.

As wrong infects society it is an inevitable response that with time there are people who will come to see how empty the way of life is, how hope seems to have left life, how meaningless life has become, how self centered life is. Also, how those who profess to love Christ in many cases have allowed this to happen.

No wonder so many are confused, no wonder they often look elsewhere for some meaning to life. As people look for something else the religions with strict moral and spiritual codes appeal because within the person is an emptiness they do not want to have and they believe that these strong faiths may help them fill this inner void.

Because these people have not had at times a clear guidance to the Christian and Catholic faith it is unknown to them that within Catholicism is all they need in the love of Christ. That within the Catholic Church resides the true, the best and the clearest instructions from God Himself on how to live a good and truly peaceful life. Also, as some may not have had the examples of sacramental lives set before them by their family and friends these unfortunates are blinded to the fact that on earth a person can come no closer to God than in the Holy Sacraments of the Holy Catholic and Apostolic Church.

Now in the sadness and confusion of the evil that has permeated society these poor souls, for that is what they are, turn from the true faith of God and embrace faiths that do not have the fullness of God's truth within them. Embrace faiths that are confused or mixed up interpretations of what God has really said and what God really wants from mankind.

Faiths that place what seems like good moral standards before people but which have limited morality in themselves. Which is evident by their denial of Christ's teachings, their denial of Christ as the only Son of God, of His death and resurrection, as the Saviour of mankind and as Divinity and Man. Faiths which rule by fear and not by love. Faiths that demand total obedience even condemning those who would leave them to death.

What a shame it is that by the pride, blindness, weakness, selfishness and apathy of some Christians others are opened to accept that which opposes Christ. Now is the time for all Catholics to reflect on how they have and are living their faith and what effect this is having not only on their family members but also on those around them and those they meet in every day life. Now is the time to start living as Christ asks and to let His gentle and compassionate love be seen in our Catholic hearts. Let us turn no more people away from Christ by our weakness. Instead let us start to bring those who have turned away back into the loving embrace of Our Lord Jesus by the strength of our living faith in all we do. Let us stand up boldly proclaiming God's love for all and invite all to find true life, true peace and true love in Him and in His good news.

LOVE IS THE ESSENCE of the Catholic faith for God is love, and so the faith He gives to mankind must be the faith of love. Today many Catholics have forgotten this and seem to live a faith of little love. The love of God is so often secondary in a person's life and the love of others is almost non-existent. Many Catholics love their wives, their families and their friends but isn't that the love most people have in the world, regardless of faith or of no faith (Matthew 5:46 "for if you love those who love you, what recompense will you have? Do not the tax collectors do the same?" 5:47 "and if you greet your brother only, what is unusual about that? Do not the pagans do the same?").

While this type of love is meant to be a part of the love we as Catholics live, it is not all there is to love. True love goes far beyond that.

True love is to love God first and foremost before self, before others; even family.

True love is to love others before self. To treat others not only as you expect them to treat you but to treat them with the love that Christ, Our Lord, has for all people; an unconditional love, a sacrificing love, a serving love, a gentle love and a compassionate love.

True love can only be lived by living in the one who is love itself, Christ, Our Lord. There has to be a complete abandonment of self into Jesus, Our Divine Lord. In that abandonment of self, a deep desire that Jesus will live in you, through you, and with you in every moment of life. That each moment of your life is a moment where you can let God's love, united with your love, reach out to touch the world.

Each Catholic is meant to be a vessel of true love bringing that love with them wherever they go and to whomever they meet. Then in living this way The Holy Spirit of love will fill the life of the person with His Divine Grace in abundance, so that the light of God's love through the person will illuminate the dark in the world.

With the power of God's gentle love residing in the heart and soul, no longer will a Catholic be a prisoner of the world, for now the things of the world are brought into perspective. With the spiritual sight that comes with true love it is seen that the worldly things are temporary and truly of little value in eternity (Matthew 16:26 "What profit would there be for one to gain the whole world and to forfeit his life?"). A person begins to see that whatever they have in the world is a gift from God to be used for the betterment of all mankind. Inside burns a desire to share what you have and not to keep for self more than you need to live for Christ.

In the lives of many Catholics this has been forgotten or is ignored and so these people do not love God or love others as they should. Many put the world first in life and the result of that is they stop truly loving.

The world leads people to love of self, not to the love of God and others. The world leads to greed and selfishness, both of which stop and deny true love.

Life for many Catholics is no longer Catholic but worldly. The Catholic life is meant to be one that, while lived in the world, lifts the person beyond the desires of the world and to desires of eternal life in heaven.

Catholics, because they have the fullness of God, the fullness of Christ in their faith, are meant to find their lives fulfilled in their faith. However, because so many have taken their focus from true love, they do not find what they should in their faith. To many the faith is just an empty shell they use to cover their failings, their weaknesses and their sins. To many the Catholic Church and its teachings come second in life to what the world says and the life the world encourages people to live. Frequently Catholics listen more to their governments than to their church, accepting the government's line before church teaching.

Some have forgotten that God speaks in pure love through His Holy Catholic and Apostolic Church and that when they do not listen to the church they are not listening to God. In not listening to God, people turn from His love, for all His teachings and commandments are ones of love. They turn their faith into one that is Catholic only in name but not in practice and not in love (Luke 6:46 "Why do you call me 'Lord, Lord' but do not do what I command?").

Some have turned their faith into a nationalistic one where it is entwined with their countries' interests, which are placed first, and distort the faith to be a shadow of the true faith of love.

The Catholic faith is not for one nation and is not based on any nationalistic ideals.

The Catholic faith is the universal faith of love for all people, where all people are seen as equal and are loved equally.

The Catholic faith is based on the teachings and ideals of Christ, as it is the body of Christ, Our Lord, and therefore is not one that can be swayed or changed by the worldly ways.

It is the same for all Catholics who are part of the Body of Christ, they too must not be swayed by the world, they too must not change the faith to suit the world or self. Each Catholic is meant to live to Christ's way of love and to no other way.

If Christ, Our Lord is truly loved, with that love would be the desire to please Him and to be obedient to His Holy Will. Within Catholicism there are people and groups who are disobedient to the church, to the Pope and to the will of God through His church.

It seems pride has blinded some so that they forget where disobedience comes from. Lucifer is the prince of disobedience. It was he who first led man into disobedience and it is he who encourages continued disobedience. Foolishly, some forget what this disobedience has brought to mankind, from the beginning it has brought hurt and suffering. Adam and Eve, in disobedience, were sent from the Garden of Eden into a world that was further from God and His love and so they suffered. Then evil introduced sin in place of love, as Cain murdered his brother Abel, whom he should have loved and not hated with jealous anger. The history of mankind continued and continues with foolish disobedience and with unnecessary suffering because of it.

With the pride of disobedience, love is denied. In that denial, those Catholics who are disobedient, weaken the church and open it to attacks from the world. They also weaken the whole of mankind by denying God's love in their own lives and then by denying others who would have been touched and benefited by that love in them.

How Lucifer laughs at the foolish pride of some Catholics who deny God's love and put love of self and their own desires before God. These Catholics do not imitate Christ, who was totally obedient to the Father's will, instead they imitate the prince of pride and disobedience. Sadly so often they do not even recognize what this may cost them in eternity (Matthew 7:21 "Not everyone who says to me 'Lord, Lord' will enter the kingdom of heaven, but only the one who does the will of my Father in heaven.").

Every Catholic who truly wants to be a Catholic, who truly wants to be an imitator of Christ, must live in loving obedience to God, to His Holy Catholic and Apostolic Church. They must live a life of true love where they deny themselves for the love of God and for the love of others. This is the faith that The Lord Jesus gave to mankind and this is how all are meant to live if they want to live in His eternal glory in heaven.

MY DEAR FRIENDS, I would like to share with you in my own words some of the things The Lord has been sharing with me in recent times in regard to the poor and needy in the world and how the affluent often ignore them or do so little to help them.

There are many people who desire to help the poor knowing it is part of their love of God and of fellow man.

How can a person claim to love God if they do not love those whom He loves and whom He created? Love of others is an essential part of the Catholic Faith. So then if we love others how can we look upon those in need and not reach out in love to help them, as not doing so is to stop loving and to deny love in life.

How can those who claim to love God see themselves as more deserving than others and turn away from those in need, thinking or saying, "it is their own fault" or "let someone else help them"?

Today people make many excuses for not helping the poor and for keeping what they have for themselves. There are many listening to the secular world before The Word of God and follow the way of greed, waste and selfishness. Today many of those who are part of the Catholic Church... which is the fullness of Christianity...and also many other Christians live a worldly faith focused on their own needs and desires, placing these before their faith and are blind to the fact that they do so. Society in many countries has drawn the faithful away from the faith and into self so that no longer can they be called faithful.

How many Catholics, how many Christians in the wealthy countries, when they see the poor and those who suffer with no means of overcoming their suffering, have an ache within their heart to help, a longing to reach out and comfort those in need or despair, a burning desire to do all they can to alleviate the suffering?

Many have become so used of seeing the poor, the needy, the suffering on news reports that they take little notice.

So many see the hurt of the poor with eyes that are blinded to the people and think only for a brief moment about what is happening, maybe hoping this will never happen to them.

So many from affluent countries believe it is their right to have a comfortable life and think only of the happiness and joy that they can find in life for themselves or maybe for their close family and friends.

Some people have forgotten that God gave all to mankind and he gave it to be shared equally by all. Some have forgotten that they are meant to share and have been seduced into the selfish ways of the world through their pride, desiring to keep what they have and desiring more and more for themselves.

These foolish people either do not realize or do not care that they have more at the cost of others who have less. Others who have their lives, their countries, and their communities exploited by the wealthy nations. Others who work like slaves for little or no wages. Others who give their lives in dangerous conditions as they toil to keep the wealthy happy.

Then, with the arrogance of the evil that blinds them, the people of the wealthy countries waste in large amounts that which would feed the poor, which would give those in need much of what they require.

Now is the time for all to reflect on how they live, how they waste, how they use more than is their fair share of

God's gifts to mankind. Now is the time for all Christians to actually start living as Our Lord, Jesus asks us to and not keep living to the ways of self-centered society.

Let us not use more than we need. Let us not take advantage of others. Now let us do what Christ Our Lord calls us to and that is to love and always to share with and to care for others.

Let us not do this in false ways that are there only to ease our consciences or make us feel better but let us do these things in true love of God and fellow man. It is not uncommon to hear Catholics say they fast on certain days which is a great spiritual blessing. However, some of these same people when the clock strikes one minute past midnight stuff themselves with food, eating what they missed out on the previous day, what sort of fast is that? When a person fasts and feels hungry they should think of those who feel hungry every day because they have no food. Then think of how they can help these poor people.

To fast is a wonderful way of opening oneself up to God in sacrificial love. However, the fast should be a true sacrifice, not just something that is done to make a person feel they are holy, or something they do because others are doing the same, or to get attention for themselves.

In Holy Scripture does it not say that when you fast not to let others know and not to let everyone see how you suffer for God.

Matthew 6: 16–18 "When you fast, do not look gloomy like the hypocrites. They neglect their appearance, so that they may appear to others to be fasting. Amen, I say to you, they have their reward. But when you fast, anoint your head and wash your face, so that you may not appear to be fasting, except to your Father who is hidden. And your Father who sees what is hidden will repay you."

How many times have you heard someone tell you they fast!

Also it would be far better when a person fasts to put aside the money saved from the food they did not eat and give it a church charity like Caritas to be used to feed the hungry. Doing this brings tangible as well as spiritual benefits to others in need through the fast. It is important that any monies given be given only through Catholic Church organizations like Caritas and not to foundations or projects set up by lay people or secular charities as these often keep most of the money for themselves for "administration costs" etc.

The call from Christ today is the same as it has always been and that is not to think of self first, but think of God and of others before yourself.

This call is the complete opposite to the call of the world but it is the call we should all listen to if we are to truly be followers of Our Lord, Jesus Christ.

God bless you all,
Alan Ames

Iraqi War

TODAY THERE SEEMS TO BE a lot of uncertainty and confusion amongst Christians and especially Catholics as to the Iraqi War and whether or not to support peace or war. As Christians, it is important that we place Christ Our Lord and His teachings above all else, even our human loyalties, just as the early church did and just as the saints and martyrs did.

When Our Lord came to earth He proclaimed peace, love and forgiveness. Today, however, many people claim the times and situation to be different. How different are they? At the time of Our Lord the Romans occupied the Holy Land. Many were killed, tortured, enslaved or oppressed by the Romans or their puppets. The Zealots and others hoped the Messiah would come and free them from this and bring them to victory over their enemies. However, Our Lord Jesus came and proclaimed peace, love and forgiveness, not force of arms. He taught this clearly: Matthew 5:39 "But I say to you offer no resistance to one who is evil. When someone strikes you on your right cheek turn the other one to him as well." Matthew 5:44 "Love your enemies." Luke 7:27–29 "But to you who hear I say, love your enemies, do good to those who hate you, bless those who curse you, pray for those who mistreat you. To the person who strikes you on one cheek offer the other as well."

These teachings with the commandment "Thou shalt not kill" appear to be some of the hardest for people to obey or follow. Often, like the Pharisees, Sadducees and Scribes, we make clever arguments to justify ignoring or changing our understanding of what God has said to mankind. Some claim that when The Lord chased the money changers from the temple using force He gave permission for us to use force against others. However, Our Lord did not kill these people even though with one word He could have done so. Instead He stopped the wrong they did, giving them then the opportunity in the rest of their lives to reflect on His actions and words.

Some quote the Catechism teaching on a just war but the Pope has said he will not bless this war as just. There are those who look to the great Saints Thomas Aquinas and Augustine and use their words as justification for war. When Jesus Our Lord was confronted by the Jews over divorce they used the words of Moses to justify divorce. Yet Jesus replied: Mark 10:5 "Because of the hardness of your hearts he wrote you this commandment." Would Our Lord be saying this today to those who try to justify war by the words of Saint Thomas and St. Augustine?

The Vicar of Christ, his Holiness Pope John Paul II stated he was, "firmly opposed to and would not bless as just" the Iraqi war. Yet, many who claim allegiance to the Pope say that the Pope did not say the war was unjust and use this to claim it to be just or just plainly ignore his words.

Some people believe that we must respond to evil with force of arms yet, Our Lord, by example, showed mankind another way to respond to evil. When He was abused, tortured, crucified and killed Our Lord only responded in love and forgiveness. Even though the Son of God had the power of heaven at His command and could have called on that power to destroy those who were treating Him so, He did not. Instead He gave us the example which as Christians, as imitators of Christ, we are called to follow. Our Lord gave His life in love knowing it was this that would overcome evil. He showed us that we

121

must be prepared to do the same in our lives if we are to be like Him and that we should not respond violently to violence.

Our Lord also, when He opened His arms on the cross in love, opened a way for us to reach a deeper level of spirituality and higher levels of grace. In imitating Christ, Our Lord, by answering evil only with love and forgiveness, we can be lifted through the cross to a spiritual level of freedom which brings us to be grace-filled vessels of God's merciful love. This grace frees us from the chains of fear, as now in that grace we come to understand the power of God's sacrificial love. The power that nothing or no one can overcome. Filled with this power the fear of death is taken from us and we come to see that this life is part of our eternal life in Christ, Our Lord; that this life, though valuable, is only a moment in eternity, a moment to be lived for God so that the remainder of our eternal moments will be with Him in heaven.

With this realization comes the understanding that to cling to this life is futile and that while treasuring this life we should not be afraid to lose it for Christ Our Lord. Now without this chain shackling a person to the worldly life the spiritual realm opens up as the scales fall from their spiritual sight. Now it becomes clear that even if it seems as if evil is victorious, it is not. Now one can see that even if the whole world is one day ruled by those who deny Christ this will only be short lived for the power of His victory will bring His glorious kingdom to earth regardless of the opposition to it. Now it becomes obvious God's victory does not depend on us, that instead we are called to be part of His victory by uniting with Him in His sacrificial love. Eyes are opened to see that if we imitate Our Lord by submitting to the all powerful will of the Father unto death, we can be lifted on the cross with Christ, Our Lord, and that then through us His grace is poured out to touch and bless many others bringing them to salvation in Him.

Today the fear of terrorism, the fear of our Muslim brothers and sisters ruling the world, the fear of evil, leads many to justify acts of war, to justify force of arms and to justify the taking of life. These fears trap many and many in fear deny themselves the opportunity that the saints and martyrs have embraced in the past, the opportunity of being lifted high in the grace of God. In denying themselves this grace they also deny others who would have been touched by that grace through them. In denying this grace pain and suffering is allowed to grow through the evil in the world that is not now confronted by the sacrificial love of the imitators of Christ.

I encourage all Christians to consider what Christ calls them to and to answer that call in becoming sacrificial lambs of love prepared to give their all for Christ in spreading His love, His peace and His forgiveness. Just as He gave His life for us proclaiming love, peace and forgiveness to all, we too must proclaim peace to the world, not war.

May the peace of Christ be with you all.
Alan Ames

Postscript—A Message from Jesus:

"The winning of an unjust war does not make it just."

DEAR FRIENDS, In this time of bloodshed in the Middle East the Holy Father has called for all Christians and all people to unite in prayers for peace. The Holy Father in this call re-emphasizes the power of prayer, which today so many have forgotten or do not believe in.

Sadly today many see force of arms, the killing of others and the inflicting of violence upon others as the way to achieve peace. How foolish this is for true peace will not come from these ways. To support these ways is to support what goes against the teachings of Our Lord and Saviour, The Prince of Peace, Jesus Christ. As Catholics, as Christians, we should be embracing only the ways of Christ and not the ways of the world or the ways of other faiths. As Christians we are meant to be emissaries of peace in the world. Talking of and showing peace in all situations, so as to bring the peace of Christ into the world through our faith. Our support in all situations should be the support of peace and the rejection of violence, not the support of one or another cause or nation that embraces violence. When a true Christian sees others suffering their hearts should be yearning for that suffering to cease, not making excuses to justify it continuing. A true Christian would not see one race of peoples lives as less valuable than others but they would recognize in all the wonderful gift of God's creative love and would see all lives as equal in value.

In many countries today Christians have forgotten or been blinded to what it is to be a Christian and in this blindness no longer follow the peaceful ways of Christ, Our Lord, but instead follow the warlike ways of the world. If this were not so then the nations would be filled with Christian voices calling out for this bloodshed to end but sadly there is a great silence instead.

Let our prayers be for peace in the Middle East and that all Christians can make their whole lives living prayers of peace for the whole world.

May God's peace be with you.
Alan Ames

A Letter In Response To A Disagreement Of Faith

7th March 2005

DEAR [...], It was a great pleasure to talk to you however briefly in [...]

I always enjoy talking to [...] who are certainly very well informed people. I would also like to thank you for your work and the great blessing it is for the world.

I thought I should write to maybe clarify any misunderstandings we may have had in our brief discussion.

It seems we have slightly differing views on the Arab world and how to approach Muslims in the name of Our Lord Jesus.

If I understood you correctly you believe that the west must confront the Muslim world even using force of arms to overcome them if necessary.

I see things a little different in that I think when we approach the Muslim world it must be done in the same way that we confront all people. That is in the same way that The Lord Jesus did and calls us to do; the way of love and forgiveness.

It is only in the love of God we can truly convert hearts and bring others to the fullness of God's truth. It is impossible to change people's hearts with force of arms this can only happen by the force of God's love.

You suggested that love will not work on many Muslims and that to talk of God loving them would only enrage them. This is not my experience as I have discovered by the grace of God that it is His love that they long for deep in their souls.

Most Muslims seem to have more a fear of God because they have not been told of His love and it is when this Divine love is revealed to them that many open their hearts in another way to God and experience Him in a more intimate way. When I speak to Muslims, as some attend my talks in various countries, most are surprised to hear God loves them and most are happy to learn of this, of course there are always exceptions.

We as followers of Christ, Our Lord, should always try to live as He lived, showing love to all unafraid of their response to His love. We too have to remember the words of St. John, (1 John 4:7–21) where St. John tells us clearly that God is love and to remain in God we must remain in love and that we must love others, for when we do not then we cannot say we love God. St. Paul in Corinthians also reminds us that a faith without love is an empty faith and that the greatest of the gifts is love. (Of course I do not need to tell you this as you know Holy Scripture very well).

It is when we stop loving in our faith and loving and forgiving others that we allow evil to work through us in sometimes subtle or even large ways. Sometimes our living to God's way changes as we no longer imitate Christ but rather live a worldly faith thinking more about what is happening in the here and now instead of looking to the eternal life to come. It is easy to focus on the world and then to see the solutions to the world's problems in worldly ways. However this is not what Christ, Our Lord showed us. He guided us to always look to heaven and to live the way of the Father, obeying His commandments and living to them regardless of the cost or pain this may bring us.

You said in our discussion that the words of Jesus, Our Lord, were fine in theory but that we could not always live to them today. The reverse is the truth, yes, we can and must live to them no matter how hard this may be for if we say we follow Jesus we must follow what He said. To do anything less is to deny The Lord and to deny His will. It should be remembered also that Jesus knew exactly what life would be like in the future and did not say just live to My words when it is appropriate, He said to try and live to them always.

We disagreed on war with you thinking it necessary to defeat the Muslims and saying the Iraq war was just. Yet, every college of Bishop's including the USA college, declared the war to be unjust and now the church it seems is reviewing "Just War" to see if this can ever be valid. Sadly many Catholics preferred to listen to their governments and the world than listen to their church and their God. The results are obvious today. As Catholics we are meant to be obedient to the church even when we do not understand the church's reasoning or do not agree with it.

(Matthew 5:39 "But I say to you offer no resistance to the one who is evil. When someone strikes you on your right cheek turn the other one to him as well." Luke 6:27–29 "But to you who hear I say, love your enemies, do good to those who hate you, bless those who curse you, pray for those who mistreat you").

Also St. Paul confirms this (Romans 12:14 "Bless those who persecute you, bless and do not curse them." 12:17 "Do not repay anyone evil for evil." 12:20 "if your enemy is hungry feed him. If he is thirsty give him something to drink." 12:21 "do not be conquered by evil but conquer evil with good").

It is not my intention to judge or unfairly criticize you in any way and so I just write to correct any misunderstandings we may have had, hoping to clearly show what it is we are called to live to as Christians and in obedience to Our God and His Church.

Our faith is founded on Christ's words and teachings and even when they are not popular or do not agree with what the world is promoting we must live to them.

The theory of His words must become fact in our lives and must be seen in all we say and do otherwise we truly are not following Him but only following our weaknesses.

I know also you do great work for the Church and you have some interaction with Muslims and so I would suggest you read Hilaire Belloc, "The Great Heresies" who in his great knowledge of the Muslim faith shows that it truly is a Christian heresy.

It would be good to read Essad Bey, "Mohammed" where you will find it reported that Mohammed called for the conquest of the Christian churches on his deathbed.

While Muslims, like all people, have the inner soulful desire for God this does not mean the God they are reaching out to is the right God. However, this does not stop the true God reaching out to them in their limited knowledge.

Many Muslims are living holier lives than many Christians but they are living their lives in serious error. The God they know is a mixture of a pagan and the true Judeo Christian God. So as they reach out to God often they reach out to the wrong god.

The pagan moon god is very apparent in their faith, with his sign the crescent moon on their flags, with Ramadan beginning and ending on lunar events and the fasting during the day but feasting through the hours of darkness. So to say their God is the same God as ours does not tell the full truth and hides the confusion within their faith.

I am sending you a copy of one of my books, *Salaam Shalom* which has been well received by Muslims and Christians in the Middle East. I hope you get time to read it.

I pray that Christ Our Lord may be seen in you by everyone who meets you or hears you.

God bless,
Alan Ames

THE WORLD IS IN DESPERATE NEED of prayer, for today lives are being overwhelmed by evil. The evil of terrorism that attacks and tries to destroy. The evil of immorality and secularism both of which are truly terrorism of the soul. The evil of greed and selfishness, which truly terrorizes the poor.

Many people believe that force of arms or the forcing of their will or their faith on others are what will overcome these evils but history shows that is not so. If it were so we would not be in the mess we are in today around the world.

Now is the time to take a different approach, an approach that The Lord Jesus has always been calling mankind to; the approach of prayerful love.

Prayer, which is so often dismissed as being of little help or rejected because it is not something tangible, is truly one of the most powerful weapons God gives to mankind. If we want peace to come to earth and morality to return then all of us must unite in prayer for this to happen.

We must now make a special effort to pray each day for the conversion of non Christians for it is in this conversion the truth of the way to live becomes clear.

Pray for the terrorists to convert, pray for those who do not know God to convert, pray for those of all religions to convert and pray for those Christians who do not know the fullness of God's truth on earth to convert.

Let our prayers soar heavenward as an offering for all mankind knowing that as our voices are lifted to heaven all of heaven will unite with us in this call for conversion.

Let our prayers echo in eternity as we call on the one true God to bless and convert mankind to the truth of His Trinitarian love.

If all the followers of The Lord Jesus will unite in this prayer then through those prayers His divine grace will pour out over the world and change it for the better. Each one of His followers is called to persevere in this prayer for mankind and not to give up in the short term when it seems nothing is happening. We must persevere and in doing so we show that we trust in God to do what is needed. The battle will be hard for when you confront evil with Holiness then evil roars in anger as it knows in time it will be overcome. However, do not be afraid for God is with all of us and God will be there to protect us and to strengthen us when our hearts are weak.

Each one of you can find that strength in the Eucharist and each one of you can find the grace you need to persevere in the Eucharist. It is important too, that each person frequently offers the Holy Eucharist for the conversion of mankind.

Let us all embrace now what we should have been doing anyway as part of our faith, let us embrace God in prayerful love of others as we call on God in love to convert the hearts and souls of all people.

Ask your prayer groups, ask your friends, ask all you know to join in this truly Holy war against the terrors of evil in the world today.

When large numbers of The Lord's followers unite in prayer in this way who can stand against it?

Heaven is calling, are we going to respond?

May God bring each one of you to holiness in Him.
Alan Ames

COMMENT ON RECENT POPULAR SECULAR BOOKS

THERE IS GREAT interest in witchcraft being created today among not only children but the population in general by books which appear to most to be good harmless fun. However, all should be aware that in witchcraft, in the ways of darkness, truly there is no goodness and there is no true fun. These books encourage people to accept what is basically evil and to see no wrong in that. It must be remembered by all that witchcraft goes against the teachings of Christ and opposes the goodness of God.

Witchcraft brings people back to the old pagan ways, the old magical ways and the old evil ways.

Anyone who believes this is not so should look carefully at what these books contain for in them are the actual words of spells which are words calling upon evil. People should also think carefully who would know these words and write them down and why!

Now I am sure many people will say these books are harmless and that my comments are to be ignored as foolish and uninformed but isn't it those who read of the dark and see no wrong in it that are foolish and uninformed?

Evil uses what appears to be good to spread its ways for if it came out in the open and showed it's true self most would reject or ignore it. However, when evil packages itself in children's stories or in stories that seem to be of little harm it is readily accepted by many.

These books bring more people to accept evil's ways and to be led into evil's web of deceit and wrong. Interestingly when web sites are found on the internet for some of these books one finds links to sites promoting witchcraft.

Let every Christian clearly understand that when they read these type of books they read what opposes their faith, what denies Christ, Our Lord and what will bring no good into their lives.

Discernment is needed by those who are Christian so that they can see the wrong and stand against it and not accept it, as in the acceptance Christian's help spread what is against the teachings of Christ, Our Lord and help bring confusion into the lives of many.

Galatians 5:19–21 "Now the works of the flesh are plain: fornication, impurity, licentiousness, idolatry, sorcery, enmity, strife, jealousy, anger, selfishness, dissension, factions, envy, drunkenness, carousing, and the like. I warn you, as I warned you before, that those who do such things shall not inherit the Kingdom of God."

Catechism of the Catholic Church:

> *2117 All practices of magic or sorcery, by which one attempts to tame occult powers, so as to place them at ones service and have a supernatural power over others—even if this were for the sake of restoring their health—are gravely contrary to the virtue of religion. These practices are even more to be condemned when accompanied with the intention of harming someone, or when they have recourse to demons. Wearing charms is also reprehensible.*
>
> *2138 Superstition is a departure from the worship that we give to the true God. It is manifested in idolatry, as well as in various forms of divination and magic.*

Disasters

It has been a sad Christmas time with the massive loss of life due to the Earthquake and following Tsunamis in Asia. To see so much suffering and loss of life truly has been a painful experience for me as I think of the hurt so many families have to endure.

As I read some of the Christian news sites I see some are suggesting that this is a sign of the "End Times." It seems many have forgotten that disasters have happened before and will happen again and think that anything that goes wrong now is a sign of God's displeasure with mankind and the way it is living away from Him.

While it is true that the way we live is not the way God wants us to this does not mean that He pours out disasters upon mankind because of this. God has warned mankind that if it lives away from Him it will bring disaster upon itself, "Court not death by your erring way of life, nor draw to yourself destruction by the works of your hands. Because God did not make death, nor does he rejoice in the destruction of the living." (Wisdom 1: 12, 13).

In recent years scientists and others have been warning the world that events like these will happen if we do not change the way we live and stop exploiting the planet. Sadly, some countries and people have taken no notice of these statements. We were meant to be stewards of the world treating it with respect not just using it for our own advantage and to make a profit. In our blind pride we prefer to see disasters as some judgement from God rather than see them as the price we may pay for our foolishness. I wonder how many governments and people will change their wasteful ways because of this? I wonder how much more attention will be paid to the planet giving it the care and attention it needs? It seems the almighty dollar or the comfortable way of life for some is more important than the planet we live upon, the planet which God gave to us as a gift to be treasured, not abused. Mankind brings so much disaster upon itself and is so blind it cannot see this! Look at the number of nuclear bombs exploded in the areas close to this most recent disaster and what effect they may have had.

What good does it do to say everything that goes wrong is God's hand at work? Doesn't this only lead us to think little can be done by us or, as so many do, blame it on others and their sinful ways while forgetting the wrong we do ourselves.

Some also try to use these "signs" of ways to frighten people back to the faith or to accept the faith. A faith forced upon another through fear is no faith at all and once the fear leaves so often so does the faith. Faith must be brought to others through encouraging love.

These disasters should be signs to all Christians to stand up and proclaim the love and mercy of God and try to lead others to Him through the difficult moments. These disasters are times where Christians can open their loving hearts generously to show the love of Christ to the world by helping those in need. Giving generously of prayers, of time, of money, of support and of self. It is in these moments the heart of Christ should be seen clearly by all in the world as Christians stand up in His love to bring His grace to all in need.

Even if these disasters are the signs so many believe them to be or hope they are, we should remember what Our Lord said and not be afraid "But when these signs begin to happen, stand erect and raise your heads because your redemption is at hand." (Luke 21:28).

God bless,
Alan Ames

CHRISTMAS MESSAGE OF 2005

THE BLESSED TIME of Christmas is upon us once more and once more in this time we are called to remember the great act of humility by God where he lowered Himself to come into this world as a man child.

In this glorious time The Lord united heaven and earth in His divine being and His divine love, bringing reconciliation to mankind in Himself.

At His birth when He was placed in a manger, where the animals eat from, in this act the Lord was showing that He is the food for mankind to eat of so as to find full and eternal life in Him.

Already from the beginning of His life on earth He was showing us how we should live if we want to be imitators of Him as a Christian, humble lives full of the love of God and the love of all mankind.

How our Christian lives need to be ones of reconciliation bringing people together in His love and how we to need to be reconciled with God in the Sacrament of Reconciliation where God Himself waits to forgive us.

How to live in Him we must eat of Him in the Eucharist and in doing so find our souls fed with what they truly need which is the food of heaven and not the things of the world.

The message of Christmas is a message for all and all need to hear it. Today, sadly, many of Christ, Our Lord's, followers do not share this message because so many have little interest in it and instead embrace the ways of the world making this sacred time nothing more than a holiday, where they focus on pleasing themselves in having a good time. A good time that leaves Christ truly on the outside.

This holy time has become devoid of holiness for many and has become just another vacation that is seen of equal value as such things as Thanksgiving or Halloween.

This Christmas let us all begin to celebrate this great time focusing on the baby Jesus and on bringing His good news to others.

Let us turn from the frivolity of the worldly ways of gluttony, greed, selfishness and waste and turn to living and celebrating this time in holy ways.

Let us also in imitating Christ turn to those in need; the lonely, the poor, the beggars on the street, the hungry and the suffering and help them as much as we can. It is in this giving to the needy that a person truly gives in the spirit of Christ, Our Lord.

Let us all enjoy Christmas but enjoy it in the right way, the way that is Christ centered and not self centered.

The way that puts others before self.

The way that cries out joyfully to the world, "The Saviour has come" and let no one stop us doing so.

Merry Christmas,
Alan Ames

I WOULD LIKE to share a beautiful message from the Archangel Gabriel about Christmas. This is found in the book *Heavenly Words*.

ARCHANGEL GABRIEL   23/12/97

In the air was an excitement carried by the wind across the land.

In the air was a feeling that soon something miraculous would happen.

In the air was the knowledge of creation that God was coming to earth.

The people, the animals, the plants, the water, the air, the earth itself waited on the birth of the Saviour, and waited for God's only Son to bring God's glory to earth.

The whole planet waited to share in the first breath God took on earth—a breath of love that would renew this faltering world and would be the beginning of a new paradise for all.

CHRISTMAS MESSAGE OF 2006

DEAR FRIENDS IN CHRIST, With the Holy time of the birth of Our Saviour, Lord, and Master, with us again I would like to thank you all for your support and your prayers which I always need in doing God's Holy will.

As all who follow the Lord know it is a difficult time to live the faith as the world tries to lead people away from God and into self. Even in this Holy time people are encouraged by the world to think more about their enjoyment, shopping and what they will receive instead of focusing on the true message of Christmas.

As Catholics, which is the fullness of Christianity, we are called in this time to think about why God came to earth. What He offered and continues to offer to mankind. How much He loves mankind and how His life showed His love. How as Catholics we are called to a full imitation of Him in offering ourselves in love to all so that His love can be seen in our lives.

In this Holy time it is good to reflect on how God came to those of whom many would reject Him, seek to harm Him and finally take His life. Through this reflection it should then be apparent that if we are to live as He calls us to, at all times not just in this time, we too have to be prepared to go out to those who reject The Lord and in our lives for Him show them the truth of His love.

Just as the Lord came into the world as a sweet innocent child, we too should go out to the world with a sweet innocent child-like love of God and others.

Just as the Lord was not afraid to show His love neither should we be.

Just as the Lord prayed for the people of the world to accept His divine truth so should we by making our lives prayers of love unafraid of the consequences of doing so.

Today so many catholics are afraid to spread their faith, afraid to speak of Jesus, The Lord, and afraid to truly follow in the footsteps of The Son of God.

Let our gift to The Lord on this celebration of His birthday be our commitment to do His Holy will, taking His love out to all in actions, in prayers and in a total devotion to Him.

Let us pray for all to be converted be they Muslims, Jews, Hindus, Protestants, Atheists, Agnostics and yes even those who follow the evil one. Let us pray for everyone.

Let us show in our actions to all people we are totally committed to The Lord and in love of Him that we are unafraid of the world and those who would seek to stop us.

Let us show how devoted to Him we are by devoting our lives to serving Him and serving others so as to bring them to the fullness of God's love.

This Christmas we should now seek to give ourselves as gifts to God and to others instead of expecting gifts from Him and from others. It is when we truly do this then we can be confident that God will, by the power of His Holy Spirit, give us all the gifts and graces we need to live as He asks.

My hope this Christmas is that I, like all of you, can do this and in doing so can be a true follower of The Lord Jesus, God's only Son, Who, with the Father and The Holy Spirit is truly one.

God love you,
Alan Ames

THE GIFT OF CHRISTMAS

JUST AS THE MAGI CAME bearing gifts of love for Our Lord, Jesus, and came in adoration of Him we too are called to come to Him in a similar way. Our gifts of love offered to Him in love should be our lives, our hearts and our souls. This offering should be one of complete submission to His will asking only that He does with us as He desires. In doing so realizing that the Holy Child of Bethlehem, The Son of God, will bring our lives to shine brightly in Him so that we can be the new star that leads all to Him. Knowing that by His divine grace our hearts will become the hearts of love they were created to be. Hearts that will show the tender love of The Lord to all we meet. Being aware also that in the giving of our souls to Him that The Spirit of Divine Love, that The Son of God gifted His followers with, will fill our souls and set fire to them with a deeper love of God and of fellow man.

Today most look to Christmas as a time to give gifts to family and friends but forget to give gifts to The One who is the reason for Christmas. It is essential that we as Catholics return to the true meaning of Christmas which is more than ensuring the holiday is not changed or that the media and stores do not deny Christmas. The true meaning of Christmas is that in love of man, God came to earth for all people, so that all can find eternal life and joy in Him.

We as followers of Christ must then try to do the same with the offering of ourselves to God. We should be going out reminding people of the love God has for all by living as God calls us to, living as examples of love that turns away from no one, that rejects no one and that condemns no one.

This Christmas is a time where Christians can show more than self to the world, it is a time where they can show The Child Jesus to all by taking the focus from worldly things and bringing it on to heavenly things. While it is important for families and friends to get together over this blessed time it is essential they remember why they are together and bring the Child Jesus into their celebrations making Him the centre of their celebrations. Thinking also of how all of mankind is family and how we should be friends to all reaching out to everyone in love. With a helping hand where needed, with loving words for all and with an open heart radiating the love of Christ that is unafraid to express that love to all.

Let this sacred time lead us to sacred lives and away from the materialism the world draws us into. Instead of looking to the material looking to the spiritual and mystical contained within this divine gift we celebrate at Christmas. Each one of us who professes to love God and to live to His Son's Jesus' way, should turn to God and ask Him to help us see beyond the physical and the temporal, so that we can see with eyes of faith the full gift given in the birth of Our Saviour. The gift that is eternal, heavenly and that is for all.

Let us look to Mary and see in her how she lived a holy life by giving herself completely to God. Then just as Mary, The Mother of God, cradled and nurtured the Divine Child in her love try our best to go out to all the children of God and cradle them in our hearts, with love reaching out gently to nurture the true faith in the lives of others. Just as Mary and Joseph were filled with joy as their family was made complete with the birth of The Lord, let us be joyful as we try to make the lives of all the family of man complete in The Lord, Jesus, too.

My hope is that all who say, "Merry Christmas", ask the Holy Spirit to make the Christ in Christmas touch the souls of all who hear the joyful words they speak and in the loving actions they do.

May your Christmas be truly holy and filled with many blessings and graces for you and all you meet.

AT THIS THE HOLIEST TIME of the year it is good for people to reflect on what The Lord Jesus showed in His passion, death and resurrection.

No matter how much He suffered He loved and forgave.

No matter how much pain He endured He served God and Man.

Nothing could turn The Lord Jesus from the path of sacrificial love as He knew this is the way that mankind would be offered reconciliation with God and that those who would choose to accept this reconciliation would find life eternal in the Lord Jesus' divine, forgiving and glorious love.

In this Holy act mankind was shown the depth of God's love for them, a love that knows no end but lives on through and beyond even death. Mankind was also shown that life is not meant to be self centered but God centered. That in life each person is meant to put others before themselves and become sacrificial and loving servants of God and of others, just as the Lord Jesus was in His life, death and resurrection. That in doing so each person would be resurrected in the eternal and divine love of Christ.

Sadly today this is a message that many do not want to hear as many prefer to live lives centered on self and seek to find their pleasure in the world, so often with others serving them instead of them serving others.

Many who profess to love Christ love Him only after self and refuse to live as He showed and asked of those who would follow Him.

Looking at the world today shows what living this way costs...it costs great suffering through the darkness and confusion that covers the world. Darkness and confusion that causes many to starve, to live in need, to live sad and depressed lives, to live lives of addictions, to live lives of slavery to the world. Yet, still so many Christians embrace this way of life as if there is no other way.

How foolish this is, for there is another way, the right way, the way of sacrificial love, the way mankind is meant to live, the way that is Christ's way. When people start to serve as Christ did, to love as Christ does and to truly follow what Christ said then the new covenant between God and Man will bring the peace, joy, love and happiness to all that Christ has promised. This Holy Week is a time to reflect on that covenant and to live it as a new people in Christ, Our Lord and no longer be slaves of the world but be servants of Our loving God.

Interviews

ALAN AMES, 54 years old, violent during his youth. He gets married very young to Kathryn at the age of 20 and have 2 children. He quietens down his life. He migrates to Australia where he becomes a talented sales manager. There he becomes more and more addicted to alcohol and drugs. This restarts his violence.

At the age of 40 an angel warns him:

Change your life, pray!

During the first months of his conversion he is physically and morally attacked by the evil one.

At the beginning he asks himself if he is going mad but St. Theresa of Avila confirms to him what is happening and says:

You are going to hell unless you change.

He changes his life, his wife converts to Catholicism.

He receives messages from the 3 Persons, the Trinity, Our Blessed Mother and the saints. He published 16 books. He is supported by his archbishop from Perth. He travels all around the world where his conferences gather big audiences. He has the charisma of conversion and healing. He lives painfully the Passion of Our Lord, more often without visible stigmata but blood is shed rarely.

René Laurentin [RL] You live in Perth, Australia, how did your spiritual charisma begin?

Alan Ames [AA] I was born in England, in a catholic family but I never went to church and at school I was the worst student and I got expelled from the Jesuit school because I was so bad. I was uneducated and it was just later in life when I migrated to Australia I began to educate myself and there I got a good job as a sales manager in a pharmaceutical company. I worked for that company for more than 10 years, before God came into my life. I'm married, I have 2 children, a daughter of 32 and a son of 29 and I have lived in Australia for nearly 30 years now.

[RL] Are they both established in Australia?

[AA] Yes, they both live in Australia.

[RL] When was your first locution or apparition? When and how did you perceive that?

[AA] The first was in 1993, there had been some before but I didn't recognize what they were. But in 1993 I was travelling for work and I was in a city called Adelaide in South Australia and I just arrived, got off of the aeroplane and gone to the hotel. When I was watching the news on the television and as I watched the news all of a sudden in front of me appeared a horrific looking man, a terrible looking man who began to strangle me and I thought I was going to die and there was nothing I could do to stop it, my hands went through him, I couldn't do anything. Then a voice in my head said:

Pray the Our Father!

Which I would have never thought of because I never prayed but in desperation I prayed the Our Father. When I prayed the Our Father the strangling stopped, when I stopped praying the strangling started again. So again I prayed the Our Father and it stopped. This went on all night. That was my first experience, I was terrified. The next day the voice in my head said to me it was an angel that God had sent to me to help me through these difficult times. After that the angel was speaking to me for maybe one or two months and encouraging me to pray.

[RL] Was it an interior voice or external ear?

[AA] At that time it was interior.

[RL] You couldn't hear it?

[AA] That began later, first it was inside.

[RL] Were you surprised of both: the horrible man and the interior voice?

[AA] I thought I was going crazy, I thought I was mad and I was terrified.

[RL] By hearing the good voice were you more in peace, more profound peace.

[AA] The voice of the angel brought peace and encouragement and then as the angel continued to speak to me

I felt an unusual feeling which was a feeling of love that I had never known before.

[RL] Did this first experience change your life? How did it change?

[AA] Not at all, except that I began to pray the Our Father but I didn't go to church. These experiences continued with the angel and also with the evil one.

[RL] Was it daily or weekly or monthly?

[AA] Every day, the angel would speak to me: encouraging me to change my life, to think of God, to stop living a bad life.

[RL] Did it also change your relationships with other people?

[AA] Not in the beginning because in the beginning I didn't change. I still was a bad person.

[RL] You said you were in these times a hard man and didn't immediately change, convert.

[AA] When I began to change it was 2 or 3 months later. The angel said:
You are not changing! So I am leaving you.
The angel left and then Saint Teresa of Avila came and began to speak to me.

[RL] The second interior voice was not an apparition?

[AA] When Saint Teresa came at first it was a voice, then it was apparitions. Again, when she came, I was travelling for work and again in the same city Adelaide where I had this bad experience.

[RL] Did you see her in Carmelite habit?

[AA] What happened is that I was in the hotel room and St. Teresa appeared to me and she said:

Pray, pray the rosary!

So she asked me to go and get a rosary, I didn't have any rosary beads. It was maybe 9.30 at night and I said:

Where can I get rosary beads at this time of night?

She said:

There is a shop around the corner that's opened that sells rosary beads.

I replied:

At 9.30 at night, that's impossible!

She said:

You go there!

I went thinking: it's impossible. But I got there and there was a religious shop that was open. They were doing stocktaking and I went inside and she said:

Get that rosary!

It was a brown one which was the color of her habit I saw her in, the same color. With the rosary beads I went back to the hotel room and she said:

Pray the rosary and pray 15 decades!

Which is three rosaries.

[RL] How was she? Tall, little, big? Can you describe her briefly?

[AA] Her was face hawkish, stern face. Like a school teacher, that's very strict. I didn't want to pray and so she said:

You must pray and you must pray the rosary, because you risk losing your soul!

She said that it's the rosary that would lead me closer to God. That in every prayer in the rosary, if I thought of

God it would be a step closer to God. So I had a big argument with St. Teresa because I didn't want to pray, I didn't like prayers. She won the argument. With her help I began to pray. I didn't know how to pray the rosary.

[RL] Can you give me your date of birth? You were born as an English citizen and now you are Australian?

[AA] I was born on the 9th of November 1953. I have three citizenship, English, Australian and Irish

[RL] Which are your links with Ireland?

[AA] My mother is Irish.

[RL] So you have three passports?

[AA] I have two but I can have three. But I call myself a citizen of the world.

[RL] A citizen of the world, not of little Europe. Which were your steps after Teresa?

[AA] The first thing of course was prayer which helped me to focus on God and to look to God and begin to call out within my heart for God's love even if I didn't understand what was happening. Saint Teresa and other Saints now who began to speak to me St. Stephen, St. Andrew, St. Mathew were the first three other saints. They began to encourage me to read Holy Scripture and to study the life of Jesus. Which I started to do. Then later with the saints and with our Blessed Mother Mary who began appearing and speaking to me.

[RL] After St. Stephen, St. Andrew and St. Mathew the Virgin Mary appeared?

[AA] There were more saints.

[RL] More than 50?

[AA] More than 100 now.

[RL] The Virgin Mary came before, between the 10 or 20 first?

[AA] What happened, St. Teresa and then the three saints I mentioned who began to encourage me to pray and read the Holy Scripture and to start going into church. Then our Blessed Mother Mary appeared and with the saints she encouraged me to go to the Mass more and more and to receive the Eucharist. Because it was explained that in the Eucharist I would find God and I would find the fullness of life and the fullness of my faith.

[RL] Did you see her or did you only hear her?

[AA] The first experience I had with our Blessed Mother Mary was when I had gone back to England for a holiday. I went to a church called St. Edmund's where I used to go as a child but I got caught stealing in that church by the police and I never went back to that church again until I was preparing for marriage. But then when I went back for a holiday, the saints encouraged me to go to the church and so I did and unusually for me I went to Mass. Afterwards I was in front of the Sacred Heart statue praying and it began to shine white and there before me was our Blessed Mother Mary. I was very confused because I could see her heart and it had some white roses around it. At first I thought it was the heart of the Sacred Heart statue but it was a little bit different. Now, I had never heard about the Immaculate Heart of Mary. I had never known what it was. It was only the next day when I saw a prayer card I realized I had seen the Immaculate Heart of Mary. I realized also what a great blessing it was because I saw the two Hearts, the Sacred Heart and the Immaculate Heart as One. That truly was a blessing. So the statue changed and it became our Blessed Mother and she was alive, physically before me and Her first words to me were:

Pray, pray, pray.

And so in my logic that meant increasing my prayer by three times so I began to say 45 decades of the rosary every day, which was difficult. So Our Lady said to me she was my mother, that she is everyone's mother and she loves every person as a mother loves her children. That she is there wanting to lead every person closer to God, deeper into the Heart of Jesus, the Father and the Holy Spirit. She said that's the wonderful grace that God gives to her to bring people closer to Him. That she is reaching out to take my hand and everyone else's hand to lead us to God.

[RL] When you saw the Virgin Mary, did you see the statue transfigured or the Virgin Mary herself?

[AA] The statue changed and became the Virgin herself which moved.

[RL] Can you describe her?

[AA] She was in white, shining white.

[RL] Was the light around her or did the light come from her?

[AA] Both. Blue eyes and black hair, and so beautiful. So much love in her smile. How can I describe her, it's so difficult to describe her. She may have my wife's height which is about 5 feet 6 inches.

[RL] How many times did you see the Virgin Mary? Rarely, ten times or more?

[AA] Many, many times.

[RL] Perhaps hundreds of times?

[AA] Yes but not only I, other people who have been with me have seen Our Lady or Our Lord also.

[RL] By these apparitions and locutions did the Virgin Mary play a special role in your Christian education and formation?

[AA] Yes, and she still is. I'm still learning and still being converted every day.

[RL] More than the other saints, more motherly?

[AA] Much more. She helped me to understand the love of God more, to understand the sacraments more and with Her encouragement I was drawn into the sacraments.

[RL] Is this the main apparition you have with those you have spoken to now?

[AA] In the beginning but the main apparition now is Jesus, our Lord.

[RL] Jesus appeared afterwards. Can you tell when and how Jesus appeared and spoke to you?

[AA] I think it was in 1994. Our Blessed Mother Mary said to me one day:

My Son is coming to you.

And there before me was Jesus telling me He loved me and He wanted to forgive me. Now it was the greatest day in my life, up to that time but it was also the most difficult day because I saw Jesus on the cross suffering and dying and I saw how all my sins had contributed to that, had caused that. How every time I've hurt someone I was hurting Jesus as He suffered and died. Any time I told a lie, I was lying about Jesus as He suffered and died. Every time I gossiped about people, I was below the cross with all those gossiping about Jesus as He suffered and died. I saw every sin that I did was hurting Jesus and I saw Him hanging on the cross and just loving me and calling out He wanted to forgive me no matter how much I hurt Him. I felt so ashamed, so embarrassed, I didn't want to live anymore. I fell to the ground. I was crying, I was sobbing like a baby, seeing the love of Jesus and how gentle, how wonderful He is and just seeing how I had hurt Him. I begged Him to let me die, to send me to hell because I didn't feel that I should exist anymore. I just didn't want to live, but Jesus kept calling out that He loved me and He wanted to forgive me. For five hours I was crying and crying asking God to let me die. Eventually with His grace I built up the courage to ask to be forgiven. I asked Jesus to forgive me and He said He did. At that moment it was like a weight being lifted from me. I felt so different within. I felt His love touching me inside in such a wonderful way and I never wanted to lose that again. I felt refreshed, renewed a different person and in that moment I knew that I loved Jesus and I knew I could never hurt Him again purposely, even now I do because I sin every day unfortunately. I just knew I never wanted to leave Him or be away from Him again. It was at that moment that I totally committed my life to God.

[RL] **You said that the Virgin Mary was more motherly, superior, greater than the other saints. What are the differences between Mary and Christ.**

[AA] The love of our Blessed Mother is a motherly love, that is very deep, very strong, so pure. The love of God is way beyond that. It seems to be thousands of levels higher. It's so intense, it's overwhelming. He embraces every cell in your being and when that love touches you and His presence touches you in that way it draws you into in His love and makes you One in His love. As you are absorbed into God, into Jesus, you become part of His love, you become integrated into Him in the Eucharist. It's so hard to explain the difference because in the love of God you experience complete ecstasy, complete joy, complete happiness. Where, in the love of Mary, you experience this wonderful love, this wonderful peace and happiness but it's not the total love, the total fullness of life, of happiness that you experience in God.

[RL] Christ is transcendent, divine.

[AA] I just wanted to share what our Blessed Mother and Jesus Himself explained about our Blessed Mother Mary. Our Lady said once to me that today many people are confused with the role of Mary. That many people, especially, our protestant brothers and sisters think that we go to Mary and worship her and adore her as we do with God, which is not the case. Our Blessed Mother said from the beginning that she is only here to lead people closer to God. That when we come to our Blessed Mother we join with her in prayer, in worship, in adoration of God and it's the same as being with your mother on earth, united with her praying together and loving and worshiping God. So, Mary our Blessed Mother, is there to draw us closer to God and she has always told me that she tries to get our focus to the Father, to the Son and the Holy Spirit, always leading us to look to God, to come closer to God not to come closer to her. But Jesus reminds me that Mary is the most special human being of all. The fact that she was His mother lifts her above any human that ever was or ever will be created. She had to be pure because God Who is pure love could not come to earth through a vessel that had the slightest sin on it, because then God Himself would have had sin on Him. So God in His mercy created Mary pure and with her fiat, with her Yes, she remained that way: Immaculate. So Mary is the most special human of all: the Immaculate One, but God is beyond that, He is the Divine One and Mary, our mother always reminds me of that. However, God always reminds me that we should treat His mother with the respect that she deserves and not to turn away from her but to embrace her, because in her embrace she draws us into the Heart of God.

[RL] When you have these communications with Mary or Jesus, do you always see them or is it more locutions without apparitions?

[AA] Normally 75% of the time would be locutions and 25% would be visions.

[RL] How do you see them?

[AA] In many different ways. Sometimes I see them physically, as I see you. Sometimes it's like watching a movie screen. When there is no vision you can feel the presence. But the way I see them is physically, or statues come to life, in the Eucharist I see the face of Jesus very often. I see them in many, many places and in many different ways. But the feeling in the heart is always the same. When I have the locutions I feel wonderful inside, I feel the presence and the love of God. When I have the visions I also feel the presence and the love of God, that's always there, that wonderful feeling is actually with me every moment of the day.

[RL] **This presence remains a vision which identifies us with Jesus and our Lady in the communion of saints. Are you feeling this?**

[AA] That's so true but what I find in a different way is that through the Eucharist, as our Blessed Mother encouraged me to be Eucharistic and to go to the Mass every day, and uniting with Jesus in the Eucharist, every day, that presence of His love, the presence of Him resides inside of me every moment. I know also that in union with Jesus in the Eucharist, I am allowed to reside inside of Him through this wonderful union of God and man that everyone in the Eucharist receives. But it seems in me, when I receive the Eucharist every day I am just filled with a joy that lasts all day inside of me even in the most difficult and hardest moments, still inside of me there is a peace, a joy, a happiness and this is all from the Eucharist.

[RL] **For you is the Eucharist more than an apparition?**

[AA] Of course, the Eucharist is everything. The Eucharist for me is life. If God said to me that I had the choice between the visions or the Eucharist, it's the Eucharist.

[RL] **The union is more than a vision.**

[AA] Yes, but sadly today many people, don't know this or have forgotten this. Mystical experiences and visions are wonderful but what is far greater than all of that, and is there for every person, is Jesus in the Eucharist. God giving Himself to man and welcoming man into Him. It's the most wonderful thing, the greatest gift. But sadly so many people have forgotten this.

[RL] This essential union remains even when you are in the night of faith?

[AA] The desert, maybe in a different way to other people. In my night of faith or the dark times or whatever it is when the evil one attacks me, that presence, even in the terrifying moments, that presence of God is always there and the strength of His love in the Eucharist carries me through anything.

[RL] You live in great union with God, but there are moments or lights where you feel the presence, have you also moments of night where you feel nothing?

[AA] No.

[RL] You are always in the transparence!

[AA] From the first time I received the Eucharist never have I not experienced the presence of God. Never, every day since 1993/94, every day, all day.

[RL] Because this happens frequently, the night can be very profound. Don't you suffer from ordeals and temptations of evil? In these moments what do you feel, don't you feel that God is far away when you are attacked by the evil one?

[AA] When these attacks occur, I see them as a blessing because when they happen I turn to God, I ask for his help and give myself totally to him and trust completely in him. The evil one is stupid because every time he attacks me it turns me more to God. There have been several times when I thought I would die. Once I was in Rome and I was staying in a convent near St. Peter's. I thought I would be safe there. I was asleep and I was woken up in the middle of the night being strangled. I thought I was going to die, my back was arching, I could feel the veins in my neck were about to burst. I thought I would take my last breath, I am going to die, so I said:

Jesus if this is Your will, I accept it and I give You my soul.

From the moment I said that, the attack stopped. It's always the same. So it's why I say that the attacks turn me more to God even though at the beginning sometimes I am terrified because some of them are horrible, always it turns me to God and it's a great blessing.

[RL] Physical attacks! But do you also have sometimes interior attacks like: doubts, desperation?

[AA] Yes, always, I have these attacks every day, in different ways. The evil one always works on your mind: to make you doubt, to make you despair, to make you not trust in God and always he tries to do that to me. I am never doubting in God's love for me, I never doubt in Jesus. At times I doubt in myself because I am so weak. I am stupid because I sin every day. I have bad thoughts about people. I might say something stupid, do something stupid that I shouldn't do and when I do that I despair in myself, not in God. How stupid am I to be tricked by the evil one to do these things!

I wonder how God can be so patient with someone like me, with my bad thoughts and actions but I never doubt in God. I never doubt in His love. No matter what the evil one does if I just cling to Jesus everything will be all right.

[RL] You keep always the peace of profoundness.

[AA] There is always the peace of God's love. That's the wonderful thing and that leads me beyond the turmoil of the world and myself. Sometimes I do get distracted but very quickly God brings my focus back on to Him and on to heaven.

[RL] Did you receive a mission or messages to give to the world?

[AA] When Jesus first came to me I committed myself totally to Him when He forgave me and I fell in love with Him. Jesus said to me that He wanted me to do His work and He said:

It's going to be difficult, it's never going to be easy until the day you die it will be difficult, but don't give up!

The mission was to go out and to tell everyone that God loves them, that God doesn't want to condemn or to punish people, He loves people and wants to bring them to His eternal love in heaven. It's the same message God has always given us: that if we live in a good way, eternal life with Him is ours. The message is to find that way of living. To find the true way of living, we have to live as Jesus lived. To imitate Him in obedience by being completely obedient to the Catholic Church and by living in Him in the sacraments. To go out and tell everyone there is nothing to be afraid of in God or in His Church. To encourage and invite people to love God, to love the church. To tell them that in loving God in that way it will bring graces into their lives in abundance to bring them to a full and happy life. So the message is that God loves everyone. That God wants to forgive everyone. He only wants everyone to love Him and to seek His forgiveness.

[RL] Do you also receive messages from God The Father and The Holy Spirit?

[AA] Yes, I have.

[RL] With apparition or without apparition?

[AA] Both.

[RL] In which appearance do you see The Father and The Holy Spirit?

[AA] The Holy Spirit, I see Him as a dove or flames, sometimes feeling Him as wind. My ex-boss of the pharmaceutical company that I used to work for, he wasn't Christian, he had no faith. He was sick and he came to one of my talks and when I prayed over him he felt this wind brushing over him. He was filled with ecstasy, filled with the Holy Spirit. He became a strong Catholic, now he is studying theology and he has changed his whole life. When I see the Holy Spirit, it's a dove, flames or wind and it's always wonderful ecstasy, wonderful joy and so much peace. The Holy Spirit says the same things as Jesus, that He loves everyone, that He has got graces and gifts for everyone. He wants everyone to use those graces and gifts so that they can live a good, a happy, a full life as they are meant to and help the world be a better place.

God the Father truly is our Father. He loves us as a Father. We are His children and He wants every one of us to be with Him. He's very sad when people turn away from Him, ignore Him and commit terrible sins but He doesn't stop loving anyone. He always loves us no matter who the person is or what they have done, He loves them, calls them His child. I've seen Him a couple of times and I always say He looks a bit like an American singer: Kenny Rogers, white beard and hair. That's the closest I could describe Him but He looks much, much greater than that, transcendent, without comparison.

[RL] Do you feel the messages of the Father more powerful and those of the Holy Spirit more intimate?

[AA] The message of the Holy Spirit is actually very powerful. It's like a fire burning inside you. I feel innermost the divine grace He personalizes for everyone. When He is touching me, it's not for myself, it's for everyone: for the church. Everything God gives it's not for me, it's for others.

[RL] Does the Holy Spirit enlighten you on the future of the church and of the world?

[AA] I receive messages about the church: she will come back much stronger. We are going through a difficult time at the moment but the spring of the church Pope John Paul II spoke about is happening. Many people are coming back to church.

[RL] The return of Christ: is the parousia close or far?

[AA] When is Jesus coming back? Well of course, He is here all the time in the Eucharist which is wonderful. The Lord told me not to worry about the future. He says live your faith today and the future will take care of itself because He will look after you. Just live for Him every moment and every day.

[RL] You are not worried about the future?

[AA] Too many people focus on the end times. The Lord told me:

Don't worry about the future, it's in My hands.

He's defeated evil, all we have to do is accept that defeat and not worry about the future. One of the big risks today is that many people are looking ahead and are worried about the end of the world and many people are focused on self because of this. They think maybe they need to store food or store money and evil works to make people self-centered instead of God-centered.

[RL] What is your wish or prayer for the future?

[AA] My prayer is that every person on earth comes to know Jesus and comes to love Him, proclaim His love, their faith and is not afraid to do so. Too many Catholics are silent, they don't evangelize, that's why the world is in such a bad condition.

[RL] What do you think about […] he is from […] and laïque as you are?

[AA] I don't have any contacts with other visionaries. I just focus on what God is giving me. All I read is holy scripture and sometimes a newspaper. I never comment on others.

[RL] Have you a particular message for France?

[AA] The people of France need to stand up and live as Christ called them to live, to live His way. For as they live His way and persevere in doing so then the Holy Spirit will pour out the graces through them to change the country of France, to change the world for the better.

[RL] What are the contacts with your bishop?

[AA] My diocese is the archdiocese of Perth and the archbishop is Archbishop Barry Hickey.
He's been supporting me from the beginning, from 1994. He appointed a spiritual director who checks all my writings and supervises everything I do.

ATTACK ON AMERICA
SEPTEMBER 15TH 2001

[Question] Alan, by all accounts, the United States government and NATO are preparing for war in retaliation for the attack of September 11, 2001. What is the appropriate Christian response, or in other words, what would Jesus have us do?

[Answer] Jesus tells me that we must turn the other cheek and offer love and forgiveness to those responsible for this attack on America. We, as Christians, must reach out with open arms and love our enemy. By loving and forgiving, we are living the message of the New Testament, not the Old Testament—which calls for an eye for an eye and a tooth for a tooth. Jesus is the fulfilment of the Old Testament. The fruit of the crucifixion is the ability to forgive. The New Testament tells us that we must love and forgive everyone—not kill them when we feel it is justified. Realize the difference between revenge and justice. Revenge is not of God, justice is.

Revenge killing is wrong. War is wrong. The moment we seek revenge, the instant we set about to kill our enemy—even in the name of war—we are no different from the terrorists. If we kill people—any people—we too are murderers. No exception. God's commandment that thou shalt not kill does not have such a caveat. It does not say thou shalt not kill—except in times of war. It says thou shalt not kill!

Jesus tells me the correct Christian response is to track down the perpetrators and bring them to justice—according to the rule of law. This is the only way, for it is God's way.

There lies before us the heroic opportunity to forgive. One mustn't sacrifice his own soul for the sake of revenge. No Christian should consider revenge as an option. Bombs will not stop evil, they will only fuel it. "Violence begets violence, sin begets sin and love begets love." (Message to Alan Ames from Lord Jesus 22/10/94).

THE FOLLOWING IS A MESSAGE TO ALAN AMES FROM GOD THE FATHER ON APRIL 2, 1995, WHICH DIRECTLY ADDRESSES AMERICA'S CURRENT DILEMMA:

"Thou shalt not kill is another commandment I have given to My children. Why should I give this commandment? Why should I say that to kill is wrong? The explanation is very simple; if you kill another knowingly, then you destroy My creation, a creation of love. Not only do you destroy My creation in another but you destroy your very soul, you deny yourself eternal life in heaven. There are many ways of killing and many excuses for it but whatever the way, whatever the reason, it is still wrong, it is still a sin. If you kill for justice or for what is right, this is a sin. If you kill for truth and honour, this is a sin. If you kill for revenge or for your country, this is a sin. All killing is a sin unless it is an accident, unless it was not meant to happen.
The taking of a life no matter what the reason offends Me your God deeply and it scars your soul mortally.
Those who agree to killing, whether it be through their governments in wars or in justice, carry the scars also. Those who agree to killing as an act of mercy, as an act of help for those in pain, still carry this scar on their souls. Those who stand by and watch as others kill and say nothing, by their inaction scar their very souls. Those who kill to stop killing

become the same as those they oppose, they become filled with sin. All killing is wrong, all killing offends Me your God and all killing leads you away from God."

[Question] Why does God allow such suffering?

[Answer] God does not allow suffering. He gave us free will—the choice to choose good or evil. Some choose evil. God gave mankind this free will because He loves mankind and did not want to force His Will upon us.

MESSAGE TO ALAN AMES FROM GOD, THE HOLY SPIRIT REGARDING FREE WILL:

"The joy that can be mans is the joy of God's forgiveness— mercy, love, and willingness to take man back into His arms. If man can come to understand what can be his, then sin will leave this earth, evil will disappear. It is all up to mankind with the free choice it has been given, with the love, and with the graces God has given mankind.

God will never force His will upon man; He will only guide and advise, then He leaves it to man to decide his own future. God lets man determine his own destiny. God loves man and from this love comes God's will that man may choose freely, that man should see the right path and take it. There is only one path to God and that is through His Son, Jesus, and by following Jesus' example on how to live and how to give."

[Question] Alan, could you comment on the run on guns and ammunition which has occurred in this country since the attack of September 11, 2001.

[Answer] Christians should give away their guns. Jesus did not have a gun or knife. Get rid of your weapons of death. Prayer is a weapon more powerful than an atomic bomb. Prayer and fasting demonstrates our trust and faith in God—and they can and have stopped wars. There is no other way.

[Question] Inevitably, in times such as this, people start to stockpile supplies. Is this an appropriate response?

[Answer] Ridiculous. We must trust in God to supply all that we need.

[Question] If you had the opportunity to talk with President Bush—what advice would you give to him?

[Answer] To read the foregoing and to follow God's commands. We must work to change the entire thinking of America. America, so very blessed, must share its' gifts with all countries. America cannot be biased towards one country versus another. If we are biased and, thus treat one country differently than another, it results in anger and hatred. It is such hatred that breeds the terrorists that we have seen. In God's eyes all people are equal. It should be no different for America—a country so blessed.

KVSS Radio Interview

This is Bruce and Chris McGregor on the morning show. Joining us in the studio this morning a delight, a blessing, a pleasure, Mr. Alan Ames.

[Bruce] Alan, welcome and good morning.
   [Alan] Good morning Bruce and Chris and congratulations on 25 years of marriage, it is wonderful.

[Bruce] Thank you very much. God knows what He is doing.
   [Alan] You know I have been married 34 years. A little bit longer than you but I have to smile because often God brings opposites together.

[Bruce] Oh He did!

[Chris] Oh yes that is very much so in our case. Yes, our mothers are still surprised we are together after all this time.

[Bruce] We were just talking about housework.
   [Alan] Actually housework is my favourite job!

[Bruce] I don't mind it. I like cooking too. I enjoy it.
   [Alan] That is very good that you do it.

[Bruce] Well Chris thinks so.

[Chris] I like you more and more Alan. It is so wonderful to have you here and I am personally saying some prayers that you are able...even though you got up very early to be with us today...that somehow the Lord will give you the rest you need. You have been operating on very little sleep lately haven't you?

[Alan] Yes, on this trip it's been interesting most nights I've had hardly any sleep, I don't know why, God must be giving me crosses for a reason but I just haven't been able to sleep on this trip I've been averaging about 2 hours per night for the last week, so He'll have to give me the strength, He always does.

[Chris] Wonderful, how was last night in St. Patrick's in Fremont?

[Alan] Good, we had about 400 or 500 people there, so it was good and a lovely priest there and I think we had about 10 priests hearing confessions.

[Bruce] Fr. Cordey, he's a wonderful priest.

[Alan] Yes, he is, a really nice man.

[Bruce] There's a study that came out in England, as native son of the British Isles, it talked about how Catholicism has now jumped past the Anglican Church in England for those active, practising, church attending members and I really think that's quite an extraordinary occurrence, don't you think, Alan?

[Alan] Yes, it is, there's a few reasons for it but you have to remember that England in general is a pagan country, it really is, but what's happened is the Protestant Church is falling apart. I mean it has to by its very nature because in the Protestant Church every person can have their own theology. That's why we have so many Protestant Churches forming and splintering and breaking up because Martin Luther and also Tindal, who produced the English bible, said that anyone can decide what the Holy Spirit is saying in Scripture and whatever they decide is right. So by that in itself the church would split and split and split and that's what's happening, it's just falling apart and I think it's only a matter of time before it's fragmented even more and because of that not many Protestants go to church in England.

It's happening in other countries, less and less Protestants are going to church because of different things like women vicars, homosexual vicars and things like that and many Protestants are becoming Catholic as well. There's a group of, I think they call them the traditional Anglican Catholic Protestants, there's 50 000 of them worldwide, which recently approached the Vatican to see if they can be part of the Catholic Church. Hopefully they're coming into the church which is good. So in the UK the Protestant church is getting less and less and the Catholic Church, the numbers have remained constant or grown a bit because of the Polish people and the Eastern Europeans who have got a strong faith and because of that. Also because of many Africans, there are a lot of African Catholics there and they are strong in their faith and so because of that the Catholic Church numbers have remained constant or grown a little bit where the Protestant ones have dropped.

[Bruce] It's quite remarkable the missionary work that is being accomplished by those countries that have had to really fight and struggle for their faith and going into areas where they are supposed to, what we perceive to have religious freedom, and yet from that freedom so much is lost.

[Alan] Yes, well, it's interesting because you look at the countries that are very poor or have been oppressed for many years, the faith is strong, the faith thrives in those countries. The reason is because the people don't have the focus on the worldly things that we do in the rich countries. No wonder the Pope said that secularism is the biggest threat to Catholicism, it's true because secularism is almost like a religion itself. Instead of being focused on God people are focused on things and themselves and when you're focused on self and on the world then you turn away from God. Even if you're going to church once per week or every day, if you're not focused on God all the time then you get drawn away from Him. Then the world draws you into the way of accepting so many wrongs and you see the results of that in American society and English society and other western societies, morals have gone out the window. Families are falling apart, marriages are falling apart and society is falling apart because we're not holding on to our Christian heritage.

It's Christianity and the love of Christ that gave us the wonderful society we have in the west. Now in our foolishness in these days we're letting go of Christianity and so it's natural that the civilization will start to fall apart and that's what we're seeing now. Whereas the third world countries that I go to, like in Africa, I go there a lot, and in Africa because they live a different way they're focused more on God. In their everyday sentences, just talking as they do, they often mention God. They even, in places like Ghana, have stores that will be called Jesus' Store and have taxi services that are called God's Taxi Service, so they have God in everything whereas we have God in virtually nothing in the west.

[Bruce] I know as more and more people embrace the secularism you talk about, the things such as the birth rate continues to drop off. I mean, I think across Europe we've seen signs of that secular kind of nature have taken over, things really do drop off and we're kind of teetering on that same danger zone here in America which I think would have surprised our founding fathers.

[Alan] It's interesting as well because as the birth rate has dropped through abortion and by people being persuaded not to have children and think about themselves. It's all about self, when you have abortion it's self, when you're not having children it's self because you work, get more money for yourself, nicer holiday, nicer car. Then the other big deception is get married later. Of course what happens then by the time people get married later, often they can't have children. Maybe because the woman may have been taking the oral contraceptive which has a bad affect on fertility or they are just too old to have children and that affects the birth rate. Then you have to import migrant workers because you don't have enough people here to fill the jobs. If you had the proper birth rate you wouldn't need so many migrants because you'd have the people there in those who are born.

It's so sad to see how blind people are, they keep going on about abortion and how it is a right but it is a wrong, a terrible sin and they don't realize that they're destroying the future. Look at how civilization is now, like I said it's falling apart and if you're going to kill and kill the next generations you're going to make it worse in the future. So many people complain in America how society is changing yet no one seems to do much about it, people just accept the way things are. They complain but accept and just let it go on and on. I hope that people will start to change and start to stand up and demand from their governments that there is change for the better not for the worse.

[Chris] **It's, I think, very important for people to know your background because you do come from a real clear understanding about how a lack of morality in our lives, a lack of sense of values can really be very destructive not only to ourselves but our relationships.**

[Alan] Yes, well I lived a bad life, a really bad life. I came from a really poor family in England. My mother's from Ireland and my dad's English; both Catholics. My dad was in the second world war and he had a very bad experience, he was a tail gunner in a Lancaster bomber which got shot down and he saw his best friend burnt alive in front of him...war is a terrible thing. I think there should never be war. From that he became an alcoholic and I can remember him screaming at night time in his dreams. He became an alcoholic, became extremely violent, a gambler, did all sorts of things and I think he was a role model for me because I grew up not believing in God. We never had much money, often we didn't have food. I used to look at other people and saw what they had and think if God existed how can they have things and I have nothing? I thought surely God didn't exist. I decided at an early age that the only one who would look after me was me because my dad had his problems, my mum tried to look after us but there were five boys. She didn't have any money, she was struggling, she had to go out work and it was very difficult so I decided I had to look after myself because no one else would. I began to steal, I became extremely violent, I joined one of the worse motorcycle gangs with my older brother Dermot, we were both extremely violent. I became addicted to many, many things and I committed just about every sin and I was totally absorbed in the world.

I met my wife and she didn't know how bad I was because when she met me I was a bit different to her than I was normally. Anyway we got married and she came from Australia, even though she's originally English. I went to Australia with her and when I got there I found Australians were heavy drinkers so I fitted in very well. As I said I was an alcoholic, I drank more and more, got more and more addictions and all I thought about was myself. I got a very good job through deceit, I told a load of lies they couldn't check it because I was in Australia and I came from England and so I told them all sorts of things and they believed me. So I got this wonderful job but when I got it I really did study hard because I didn't want to lose it. I went and did a university course and kept the job and I had lots of money coming in and all I thought about was getting more and more money all the time and more pleasure, more excitement and I didn't care how much I hurt others to get that, I was totally self centered. I didn't think much about my family, my children, my wife and I committed just about every sin and I was really deep in the gutter and the more I drunk the more violent I got. I was captain of the Australian team of a martial art that I did, because I'd been studying martial arts for 25 years and teaching it. I had a 4th degree black belt in the martial art I was doing and so when I'd fight I'd use that, I'd really hurt people, breaking bones and things like that.

At the time I thought it was really good to do that but it was only later when God came into my life I realized how stupid I'd been, how foolish I'd been because He opened my eyes to show me what a bad way I'd been living, what it had cost me and cost others. Now I saw that through the sins I'd committed no matter how small they were, that I opened myself up to evil and when evil comes into your life all evil does is bring pain, hurt and suffering. It was true because I saw that inside me evil had massaged the feelings of being unloved, unwanted, uncared for, being less than others, I always thought I was less than other people, and turned them into jealousy, anger, hatred. Which led me into bitterness and violence. Hurting me isn't the only thing evil did because through me it hurt others whether physically or emotionally and now I saw that I'd just caused so much pain for people in the way I lived. I saw it was stupid because now I realized that Jesus had been there throughout my life offering me an embrace of love but I just kept turning away from Him and rejecting His embrace. I saw now how life could have been so different if I had accepted Him because when Jesus embraces you He just brings peace into your life, love, joy, happiness, contentment and He gives you everything you need.

I've been living completely for Jesus now since 1994/95 and all I do is this work, nothing else and He's looked after me now for 13–14 years. He never lets me down, sadly I let Him down sometimes, I wish I didn't but it's my weak human nature but He never lets me down. Sometimes He takes me right to the edge and I think how can I survive but He always gives me what I need. He doesn't give you more than you need. He gives you what you need and there's always enough and I hope I can continue to trust in Him every day for the rest of my life.

[Bruce] Alan tell us about how that conversion began, when did that turning begin to happen?

[Alan] Often people ask me when did that conversion happen and I always say it happened today because every day is a conversion and my first prayer every morning is to the Holy Spirit asking me to offer the day to God and that this be my day of conversion. So I think if you stop doing that in life it's easy to get drawn away from God so you have to think about today and how you're going to be converted. Of course there was a time when the first conversion happened. Now I wasn't even thinking about God it was the furthest thing from my mind. I didn't even really believe in God I was just living this bad life and then all of a sudden one day I began to hear a voice and I thought that's it, I'm mad, it's the booze because you hear of alcoholics that see things. I thought it was me.

As I listened to the voice, which wouldn't go away, it said it was an angel and that God had sent the angel to me because He loved me and wanted my love. After the angel several saints began to speak and then later appear to me and the message was the same from the beginning...God loved me, He loved all people regardless of who or what they were, or what they had. His love was constant, it was there for everyone, He denied it to no one and He wanted everyone's love. He even loved the worse sinner in the world, the person who committed the most terrible sins, He loved and He wanted their love. Of course He didn't like the bad things we did but always He loved the person and always He wanted the person's love and He wanted the person to have the best life possible in Him. So, the message in the beginning as I listened to it was a beautiful message that I thought well, if this is being crazy then it's not so bad is it?

I wish everyone were crazy like this, so that's how it began and I was led into prayer, into the sacraments and into obedience to the Catholic Church.

[Chris] I have to ask you because of course your primary vocation was to this wonderful woman who accepted your hand and you've been married to for well over 30 years. What was this like for her as this began to occur?

[Alan] St. Katherine I call her. Well, she was a Protestant, she wasn't Catholic but she never went to church except she'd force me to go at Easter and sometimes at Christmas because of the kids. She knew a little about God but she told me later when she was young in the north of England, she comes from a Protestant family and a lot of the Protestants from northern England are extremely anti-Catholic and her father's that way, still is sadly, but she used to go with her next door neighbour who was Catholic to like their Sunday school Her father didn't know and she loved the nuns, she thought they were wonderful, she was given a Rosary and when she brought the Rosary home her father saw it and took it off her and told her she couldn't go there again. She was feeling sad and she said she looked out the windows in the fields at the back and as she looked out, she was only about 7, she could see Jesus in the fields, it was wonderful. Anyway, when all this began in my life at first she was a bit uncertain and maybe thought I was going mad as well. She actually went and spoke to a Catholic priest without my knowing and he encouraged her just to persevere and be patient but she became very happy because I changed from a man who was abusive, not violently towards her, I never hit my wife, but you know say and do bad things and treated her very badly to all of a sudden to a man who was showing love and talking of love. It took her a little while to come to terms with that and then she realized it wasn't a bad thing so she was happy with it.

As I was encouraged by St. Stephen to show love in my marriage at all times by inviting God into my marriage remembering that God should be the head of the marriage and if you put Him in charge of the marriage things will work out well. To remember that God is watching you every moment in your marriage and He treasures the moments of love in your marriage and He's sad when you don't have those moments, when you have the bad moments. When you think on that hurting Him then those bad moments get less and less because you don't want to offend God in any way. So as you focus on God in your marriage the love for one another grows and you're drawn closer together and that's what happened with my wife and myself we became closer together. She became Catholic, she's a very strong Catholic. She goes to Mass daily, adoration, she's a sacristan at times. She does all sorts of things in the church and so I think she's the holy one in the family because she put up with me for years and that would have been a heavy cross for anyone, believe me. Now she's such a strong Catholic and so sweet and gentle. I look at her and think there's the real saint in the family, that's the true blessing and I thank God for her.

[Bruce] You've been given such a tremendous gift. This wonderful blessing, not only to experience of course the supreme grace of the encounters with Jesus Christ and the love that comes from the encounters with His Most Blessed Mother but you've been given a concrete

experience with the communion of saints. For so many of us we kind of know that, I mean we know it, but in today's world we're kind of cynical about the experiences that occur in our own lives.

[Alan] It's only in recent times that we've become cynical. Throughout the history of the church there's always been contact between heaven and earth, it's always happened from the beginning of time, from Adam, but in these secular times they try to make us not believe these things or to think these things are crazy and not real and it's only the tangible that's real, what we understand. What pride that is to only believe that anything we understand is real and anything beyond our understanding is not real, I mean that is really big pride. But heaven has always been communicating with man and today it continues, it's no different and I meet many people around the world who have had experiences with saints, Our Blessed Mother, Our Lord and it changes their lives. Often it's personal experiences for that particular person.

In my case from the beginning I was told to go out to the whole world and share what was happening, but one of the things that the Lord showed me was that there's the realm of heaven and the realm of earth and between heaven and earth at the moment is a blanket of darkness covering the earth which is the sin that we invite. I mean the sin is so large in this world because we keep inviting it and allowing it to grow, but through that blanket of darkness there are bright lights shining and burning through the darkness and of course that is wherever the Eucharist is, wherever the sacraments are celebrated and it's also in the lives of those who are trying to love and live the way of Christ. They are lights burning in the dark as well which reach up to heaven and I always try to encourage people that through the sacraments and in their faith to look beyond the world and look to heaven. To look through this blanket of evil and look to the light of Christ. Look to the Father and the Holy Spirit and if you can get your focus on heaven then in the sacraments, in prayer, in your daily life for Christ and for others God lifts you spiritually through that blanket of darkness to experience the eternal light and it's when you start to experience in that way that you come to understand the mystical side of our faith.

Today many Catholics don't look for the mystical. Our faith is often worldly and they look to spiritual ways and spiritual exercises in prayers and the sacraments but they often look in a worldly way and a way they want rather than looking to God in heaven and reaching out to God and truly offering your heart and soul to God in all you do. It's when you pray in that way, when you receive the sacraments in that way you allow God to make that light within you burn brighter and brighter and draw you up through that darkness into the eternal light of His light and when you're lifted through that darkness that veil falls away and then you can start to experience the mystical in our faith. Because our faith is the mystical and that's the big difference between the Protestant and Catholic Church. The Protestant faith is a worldly faith. Yes it's a worldly faith because we live in the world but it goes beyond that. It goes beyond the spiritual into the mystical and sadly many Catholics have forgotten that and the mystical gets pushed aside or gets rejected because of the secular pressure on us. But if we can start looking to God in heaven and allowing Him to draw us as we seek His love and seek His presence in every moment and allowing Him to let us draw through that blanket of darkness, that fog of sin into the eternal light, then everyone can start to experience that communion with heaven where maybe the saints might whisper a word to you, maybe Jesus might, where you'll feel the touch of God's love on your heart and soul where the breath of His love is breathed into you and sets fire to your very being. Our faith is a mystical faith, it's far beyond anything they have in the Protestant church it's a grain of sand and a pyramid, that's the difference.

[Bruce] I think Alan that it's really important for us to keep a perspective on that, I think it's such a great point you bring up about the mystical dynamic of Catholicism. I had my spiritual director tell me once that God has sent prophets, we've had saints among us to learn from and why should we let the secular world lead us to believe that this is still not going to occur in this day and age. We have St. Padre Pio, he's our patron saint for our morning show and he's been very, very close to me ever since I discovered him.

[Chris] Even the message of love that was so beautifully conveyed to you by your encounter with the saints where have we heard that message? From a modern day saint, we heard that from Mother Teresa, we've heard that from Pope John Paul, it's the same consistent message isn't it.

[Alan] We're hearing it now from Pope Benedict. He is a great pope, he really is wonderful and has such a way of bringing the focus back onto the love of God and onto our faith and facing the issues. Not skirting around them but facing them in a gentle, loving way, whether it's the Muslims, whether it's the secular way, whatever it is, he's not afraid to stand up and speak gently and truthfully about what's happening in the world. He truly is a great, great Pope.

Getting back to the secular, the mystical and the worldly. The world is trying to draw us away from the mystical because as it draws us into the secular and into this worldly life then we start to think this is it, this life is it, there's nothing after this life. So that leads us to live totally for self because we want to have everything in this life now and we don't look beyond that and there's no reason not to sin. Why should you not sin when there's no price to pay, you can do what you like and people do and that's the whole point of secularism is to bring that focus onto self away from God and because of that so many people suffer.

We have to start looking beyond this world. Many people want to live to 100, 150 and they're taking all these anti-ageing things and looking for the fountain of youth, how crazy that is. If you live to 150 you're going to work until you're 149, you're going to be paying taxes until then, who wants to do that? If you live for the world, well the world is a pretty boring place after a while, there's only so much you can do, and without God the world is pretty empty. People often say to me you're so blessed you travel to many countries. I've been to more than 50 countries now spreading the love of God, but travelling after a while is boring. There are only so many sights you can see and there's the beauty of God everywhere but after a while it blends and you start to realize there's really not a lot in this world. We're here for such a brief time, a special time when we can grow in grace and come to know the love of God in a more intimate, more personal way. This life is only a moment in eternity, a blink of an eyelid and it's the eternal life to come that's really the important life. That's what we should be looking for in this life because we're meant to grow in grace to be prepared and ready for that life so that we can come to God in heaven, but if you take that end goal away of heaven, of God, of growing in grace, what's left in life? Nothing.

[Chris] It really struck me too that you would have such a message of love that would come from St. Stephen who really was of course the first martyr of the Christian faith and whose message was one of true forgiveness, when you read the scriptures because as he's being stoned he mirrors what Our Lord said on the cross where he said: "Father, forgive them." St. Stephen said: "Jesus forgive them, they don't know what they're doing."

[Bruce] That is the supreme act of love is to forgive isn't it Alan?

[Alan] The Lord told me from the beginning you have to forgive anything anyone would do to you, even if they are to kill you, with your dying breath forgive them and ask God to forgive them. Many people find forgiveness hard today. We hold onto anger, to bitterness, to hatred, resentment over small things, how foolish that is because when we do we're closing our hearts to God and closing our hearts to others and we suffer because of that. Because when you close your heart to God you deny yourself His grace and so your heart, your soul, your life suffers and it makes people miserable and depressed and not only themselves but others around them. I've seen so many families that are in turmoil because of unforgiveness and how Satan laughs because if he can stop us forgiving, he can stop us from imitating Christ. As Christians, as Catholics, which is the fullness of Christianity, we're meant to be imitators of Christ. But if we can't forgive then we can't imitate Christ because His life was one of forgiveness and in His death, with His final breath, His final words He forgave. So to imitate Christ we have to be prepared to do the same and if we don't well then we're doing the way of the world again and not the way of Christ.

[Chris] Sometimes it's so hard to forgive it's something we feel we can't do on our own but that's the beauty of that relationship with Jesus because He's right there to help us but we have to turn to Him don't we?

[Alan] God has called us to a partnership, He never expects us to do anything alone. He said from the beginning that He's here for us. Anything we need, He's got for us and any help we need it's there for us, in anything, especially forgiveness, if we turn to God and pray, ask for the grace and persevere. Not just say, God give me the grace to forgive and don't ask anymore, and expect to get it straight away. It doesn't work that way, you have to persevere and you have to play your part because in a partnership there's two. God will do His bit but you have to do your bit as well. And that's persevere in asking and then make the effort, the conscious, the physical, the emotional effort to forgive and to love. When you do that and play your part, God gives you the grace and the strength of heart, the strength of soul to love and to forgive as you should.

[Bruce] Also I think what a blessing was revealed to you, a relationship with the mystical doctors of the church essentially and of course I'm speaking of Ter-

esa of Avila that so mirrors what again our late great Holy Father John Paul II implored of us. To learn how to pray from the mystical doctors, go to them. Because I think we've had this period of 50 or 60 years where we've turned to everything else. We've gone to new-age, mysticism and even some Catholic prayer leaders have turned to that tradition and all it does is again you go inward, inward, inward. And all you find is yourself and it has really distorted the prayer life of so many and yet with the mystical doctors, in particular Teresa of Avila, and so many of them, you go inward and ultimately it takes you back out to Jesus. It takes you to Him always.

[Alan] Well, a wonderful prayer St. Teresa taught me especially when I'm struggling with myself which is frequently believe me, is "In me my weakness, in God my strength." It's a simple prayer, sometimes when I say that I cry because as you said it leads you into self and into God, well it does. In "me, my weakness", I look at myself and see how weak I am. How I can't do anything by myself. How fragile I am and how easily I can be led away from God and into sin. How I can fall down so easily every day and I realize I can do nothing by myself properly, all I can do by myself is sin and do bad things. I can't seem to do anything else but with God when I turn to Him and get His strength I can do anything good because God gives me the grace. It's not because I'm a good person it's because I'm seeking God and He gives me the grace as He would for any person. He truly is my strength and when you look to God and realize that, then you start to rely totally on Him and give yourself totally to Him in accepting all He gives you. So my prayer when I struggle so often is, "In me my weakness, in God my strength." It's a few simple words from St. Teresa that are so powerful and bring my focus back onto reality and the reality is that in me in my humanity I truly can't live properly without God and I can't be happy without God.

[Chris] It's about having that interiority isn't it? About allowing Christ and realizing that He dwells within us and the sacraments continue to nurture that don't they?

[Alan] Of course we have to be living in Christ, with Christ and through Christ, that's what we have to do and that's possible in the sacraments, nowhere else. You come to the Sacrament of Confession and get your heart and soul purified and cleansed, ready to receive the Divine One in the Eucharist. It's when you come to the Eucharist in the right way and receive Jesus in love, that then God and man unite in love and Jesus fills you with His being. So now He resides within you and as He lives in you and if by your free will you let His life in you come to fullness, then He changes your life to be a mirror of His life, to be an image of His life. Now you find it much easier to live your Catholic faith because you have Christ with you, strengthening you and guiding you, protecting you and watching over you and you have no fear.

Today fear is a big thing in the Catholic Church, many Catholics are afraid and fear is just a weakness of faith, that's all it is, just a weakness of faith. There should be no fear in our lives. Jesus showed us He overcame evil in all forms. He overcame the world in all ways and if we live in Christ Our Lord in the Eucharist then we should fear nothing but today so many Catholics are afraid. They're afraid of the end times, of the anti-Christ, afraid of Satan himself, how foolish that is. Satan has been defeated. I often say when I give talks in churches if there's one person there that night living in Eucharist, if Satan himself were to come into the church, Satan would flee in terror because he'd see the power of God in that person living in the Eucharist and he'd be terrified because he'd see the victory of Christ in that person. So why are we afraid?

People are also afraid of the world ending, the end times, and terrorism, all that shows again is a lack of faith because if you truly live in Christ you know your life is in His hands. You're not going to die a moment before He wants you to. He takes care of you, He looks after you, He protects you and you're not going to die before God wants you to unless you do something stupid to yourself. So there's nothing other people can do to you unless God allows it for the salvation of mankind or for yourself. So many people are afraid, they're even afraid to go out and share their faith and talk to others about Christ in case people will laugh at them and make fun of them, reject them, abuse them, hurt them, how foolish that is. If you live in Christ, truly live in Christ in the Eucharist, then you have no fear.

He showed me that once when I was in Ramallah in the West Bank, I was there in the Holy Land giving talks. I was very blessed to receive permission from the Latin patriarch to speak in the Basilica of the Annunciation in Nazareth and the Church of the Nativity in Bethlehem, where Jesus was conceived and where Jesus was born, a very rare privilege and a great blessing, also St. Xavier's in Jerusalem. I went back a second time as they invited me back again. On the second visit I was invited also to speak in Ramallah in the West Bank which is a Muslim town. The week before I arrived the Muslims had been going into Christian houses and dragging the men out and killing them. They'd killed about 20 Catholics and Greek Orthodox. I gave a talk in the church there, some Muslims came along which often happens when I conduct talks which is wonderful. We've had some Muslim conversions which is great. Afterwards we were in the Rectory with the priest and he provided a meal and my wife was with me with several other people there. There was a knock on the door and the house keeper answered the door and came to us with a worried look on her face telling the Father that there was a large group of Muslim men outside wanting to see Alan Ames. The priest told me not to go out there. I said to the father that I have to, this is what Jesus calls us to and I looked at my wife and she nodded and smiled and I knew that this is what Jesus calls us to. He wasn't afraid and I should not be as I go to the Eucharist daily where He gives me the strength. I'd just received Jesus in the church, and I felt full of Him and I knew I had to go out there. But I have to say as I went down the corridor and put my hand on the door, I was just about to open the door and I thought well maybe this is my last moment and I said "Lord, well if it is, it's a moment for You and thank You." I opened the door, I was expecting a shot, or a knife or something and there was a group of 30 or so Muslim men there. As I introduced myself, I was expecting to die at that moment, when one of them said that their friend was dying of cancer, can I come and pray with him, please.

So, again Jesus showed me that there's nothing to be afraid of, people are longing for Jesus' touch and we just have to look past our fears, trust in Him completely and just step out, trust in Him and He'll look after us. Even if He does call us to give our lives for Him, what a blessing because then in that we step through the doorway of death into the eternal life with Jesus, we shouldn't be afraid. Today so many people in the west, in America, are afraid to talk to others of their faith, afraid to stand up for the faith, gently and lovingly as they're meant to and all that shows is a weakness of faith.

[Bruce] I think that's a beautiful underscoring on that thought that we just came through Divine Mercy Sunday and what a powerful phrase: "Jesus, I trust in You."

It's a couple of minutes in front of 8:00 and we're here with Alan Ames. Again, Alan will be speaking tonight at St. Wenceslaus Church. It begins at 6:30, praise and worship and Mass at 7:00. Alan will then give a talk and a healing service will follow that. Tomorrow Alan will be at St. Cecelia's Cathedral with our archbishop Francis Elden Curtis presiding. He'll also be staying for Alan's talk and hearing confessions as well and we'll have more on that.

Welcome back to Spirit Mornings with Bruce McGregor and Chris McGregor joined in the studio this morning with Alan Ames. A real blessing for all us here to be able to have this amount of time with Alan who has been doing a lot of travelling and battling a little bit of sleep deprivation so we'll continue to pray for you that a restful night's sleep will come your way.

[Alan] Thank you I had to smile when you said 56 degrees and it's going to be quite pleasant, that's like winter for me in Australia.

[Chris] Some feel that way around here but it has been a hard winter in this area we haven't experienced it in a long, long time but yet there's a tremendous blessing that's going to come from that because of the snow pack we've had. We no longer will have a drought that we've experienced so isn't that something even in the hardship there's going to be blessings that flow from that.

[Alan] As I travel the world the weather everywhere is changing some people say it isn't, it's crazy to say it is, but it is everywhere I go. Even in Europe at the top of the alps there's hardly any snow and one of the glaciers is melting there. But it is a blessing in a way because many people are starting to look at the gifts God has given us in the environment and as they look to that gift they start to see God more and more and His love everywhere. Many people are being brought back to treasure the gift He's given us in this world because it's a great, great gift and we should, like all the gifts He gives, respect it and look after it.

[Bruce] **Alan, before the break you gave me** *Through the Eyes of Jesus,* **this is an audio set that you have. Do you want to tell people a little bit about this and how people can obtain a copy and then you wanted to set a little passage from this to play.**

[Alan] I was talking about the Holy Land earlier. When Jesus first came to me, maybe a year after, He started to show me His life as He walked the Holy Land, conversations between Him and the apostles, the events that happened. It was really incredible, it was like watching a movie but being there in the movie and at times being inside Jesus looking out through His eyes and experiencing some of His thoughts and emotions. At other times looking through the eyes of the apostles or the people in the crowd around or the people He was talking to. It's very hard to put into words how it happened, also at the same time He gave me the words which I wrote down as He gave them to me. It was truly beautiful. It's a book that will make you laugh and cry. It's the most popular book I have worldwide and it's changed many lives. It truly is a book of conversion. Many, many young people have converted, we've had Protestants, Jews and even Muslims converted reading this. We had it put onto CD as a speak book because we thought that would be nice and we've got a man here in the USA who works for one of the secular radio stations to record it because he's got a great voice. It's only just come out and I'd just like to play this little track for you. I hope you enjoy it.

"The sound of horses and men marching quickly could be heard and then a garrison of Roman soldiers passed us, heading for the village. The clatter of their weapons and the stamping of their feet almost deafened us as they passed. When we arrived at the village it was in turmoil. The soldiers had searched the houses for rebels and had arrested five men whom they were treating harshly. The villagers were gathered around begging the Romans to free the men. They proclaimed the innocence of the men and called for their release. The centurion on his horse would not listen and ordered his soldiers to push the crowd back. As they did a young boy broke free and ran forward crying, 'Father, father.' A large burly soldier hit the child very hard with his closed fist and the young boy, who was about four years old fell to the ground and began to convulse. The crowd became silent as the officer boomed at the soldier, 'You fool! He is only a child.'

The officer jumped from his horse and leaned over the child who had stopped convulsing and was now dead. As he removed his helmet tears were seen running down his face and he cried, 'He is only a child, a baby, my son is this age, a baby.' He began to sob from his heart. I walked forward as the crowd parted to make way for Me. The soldiers looked as if to stop Me when someone shouted, 'It is Jesus of Nazareth. The great Prophet. The great Healer.' Hearing this the soldiers stood back and I went to the child. The centurion looked at me and said, 'Can You help?' In his heart I could see a lost soul, one full of the pain of the work he did, full of death and destruction but hidden behind this confusion I could also see compassion, love and hope.

'I will,' was My reply as I leaned forward and picked up the child. 'But he's dead,' said the soldier who had hit the boy, 'There's nothing you can do now.' I gave him a soft smile and said, 'My Father who sent Me gives or takes life. It is His to command and if it is His will that this child lives then He will live.' 'Then Your father must be a magician,' said the soldier.

'No, My Father is the God of creation Who made all things and it is His will that this child lives.' As I said this the child awoke crying, 'Mother.' The soldier stood back amazed as the child's mother came back and took him, full of joy, full of thanks and praising God for His mercy. The soldiers were still staring at me as the crowd began to praise God in unison. 'Who are You?' shouted the soldier in fear.

'I Am,' I said and the crowd became silent. 'What sort of answer is that? I asked Who You are and You say, 'I Am.' 'I Am the Son, I Am the Lamb and I Am the forgiveness of God.'

The centurion jumped on his horse nervously and snapped at his men, 'Set those prisoners free! We don't want them.'

He looked with a nod of thanks and rode off leading his
men from the village."
[Alan] It's beautiful and he's got a great voice as well. I can never thank God enough for giving me this. I've probably read the books 20 times now. There are 3 volumes, yet every time I read it I experience something new and it always touches me. That's what other people say too. I have a friend up in New Jersey who came up to me one day saying that the book was a great book. That he'd been reading through it and he'd highlighted some of the parts that meant a lot to him. He opened up the book and almost every line on every page was highlighted.

[Bruce] It is a beautiful meditation and just an opportunity, we're called to do that in prayer, that whole novena where we kind of put ourselves in that place and try to experience that, try to obtain the level.

Alan will be at St. Wenceslaus Church tonight. Father Francis Valario will be presiding at 6:30, praise and worship, celebration of the Mass will be at 7:00. Alan will then give his talk and that will be followed by a healing service. It will be the same schedule for tomorrow night at St. Cecelia's Cathedral. Archbishop Elden Curtis will be presiding over the Mass also staying for Alan's talk and then hearing confessions.

[Chris] The thing that strikes me Alan especially in what we just heard, it goes back to if it is the Father's will that this healing should occur, sometimes it doesn't happen. I think of St. Bernadette who had a beautiful moment, a salvation of history for all of us at Lourdes and yet it was not for her, in her illness. Sometimes even the healing, it needs to be more than just a physical. That's the more important healing ultimately isn't it?

[Alan] As you know I pray for many people for healing and not all the healings are physical, some are spiritual and emotional. I look at St. Bernadette, she's a wonderful saint, after the Holy Land, Lourdes is my next favourite place. I love Lourdes, it's really nice. I had a wonderful experience there. I was there with a pilgrimage of maybe 700 or 800 people and after you go in the water there's no need to dry yourself, it seems that people just dry, the water just dries off. All of these 800 people who went in every one of them was dry afterwards. I went in and I was soaking wet, I didn't dry. I think it's either God is having a joke or I'm too big a sinner. St. Bernadette had a healing of course with Our Blessed Mother coming to her and drawing her to God and bringing her close to God and she was healed in that way which was different, but she suffered as we all know. However, suffering isn't something to be afraid of. Often people ask if they will be healed and I answer that they will be but I don't know in what way because I never know in what way. I really don't want to know who will be healed and who won't be physically. Often I see people who are dying and they ask if they're going to live or not and I don't want to tell them. I don't want God to tell me because it would be terrible to have to say to someone, if they don't understand death and they're afraid, to say that well yes, you're going to die, so I don't wish to know.

The healing happens to everyone but in different ways and the way they need and often it's not the way they want. If people come with say a bad heart or epilepsy and they want healing of that but then God heals them emotionally, maybe they have had bad thoughts or couldn't relate to people, having lots of arguments and bad times and He heals them of that. Maybe people have some addictions and He heals them of that or spiritually maybe we didn't know God and He brings us to know His love and of course that's the best healing...that's what He did for me. I am a diabetic, since I was 15 and before God came into my life I would have given my right arm to get rid of it, but the moment God came into my life it meant nothing. I knew the love of God, I don't care about my diabetes, it means nothing to me now. All that's important is the love of God and that was for me the great healing, to come to know His love and the diabetes well, I live with it, I know I'll live until God wants me to die. I just do my best and I accept any problems I have with that and any other sufferings I get as well and I offer it to God.

What people often don't do is when they have an illness or sickness or suffering they don't offer it to God and thank God for it. Often they're filled with self-pity thinking why did God give me this? Why hasn't someone else got this? Why have I got this or what have I done to deserve this? It's all about self, what the world draws us into. In that we actually close ourselves to God and often we actually increase our suffering as we become more miserable. That's so true because I meet lots of dying people and if you meet those who don't know God they're really miserable, hard to be around, you don't want to be near them, you're so glad to get away from them because they're always complaining and groaning. Then you meet those who know and love God and are offering their suffering to Christ on the cross and even if they're dying and in terrible pain they're so joyful, so at peace and they're wonderful to be around.

I remember a beautiful Irish priest, Fr. Sean Sorahan and he was one of the first priests who helped me after Jesus came to me and just a few years ago in Perth he was dying and he was in agony. He had a terrible cancer, he was in pain virtually 24 hours per day. The drugs that he was given didn't control his pain and he was left in severe pain. Yet he was joyful, he was happy and he was looking forward to dying so he could meet Jesus. I looked at him and thought this is a true example of a Christian, of a Catholic. This man did not care about his suffering, he was offering it to Jesus and he was offering it for others. He was so at peace and so happy, he didn't fear death, he was looking forward to death and to me that was such a great example of how to be in suffering.

[Chris] I just have to say that some of the most crippling things that can happen to us and for me, I had a major healing, it wasn't necessarily a physical healing, although I think it did have ramifications but it was a healing that came about concerning my childhood. Like you, I came from what they call around here, a dysfunctional family, there is nothing fun in that dysfunction. My father was an alcoholic and it was a very, very difficult environment to grow up in. In my 20's though he recovered from his alcoholism and really tried to be the dad that I had always wanted and once the alcohol was taken from him, that haze, allowed him to be the guy that God created him to be. He was a great father-in-law, a great grandfather but the scars from all those years for me always kind of stayed with me and it affected how I looked at things and treated people and I experienced a healing when I went to Medjugorje. There was something that happened to me there. I don't know how to explain it, but all of a sudden there was this moment where there was a catharsis of tears came out and I couldn't stop sobbing but when it was done life changed, something happened. I look back now and I look at my father and I look at those memories and they don't have the cancerous effect on me like they did and I think that type of emotional healing can be of maybe even greater benefit to your soul.

[Alan] The same happened to me, all the resentments were taken away. My father, as I said was an alcoholic, a gambler and all sorts of things and he didn't believe in God, never went to church. He died about 3 or 4 years ago and before he died I was hoping and praying that he would come to know God before he died. He was in a hospice, and about 6 months before he died he said he didn't wish to see a priest, he just wanted to be cremated. He didn't want any flowers, any religious service...nothing.

I was praying for him and saw him a couple of times and then about two months before he died, 5 or 6 weeks before he died, he called a priest in and he had confession, and communion, he fell in love with God again. He bought each of us, his five sons, a crucifix which was incredible and the nuns and nurses who were looking after him said they had never seen anyone die like my father died, he was so happy and so at peace. They said he was an example to everyone on how to die. It was because he'd come to know Christ in those last few weeks of his life, it changed him completely. It was amazing as well because he had said he didn't want any flowers on his coffin, but the day before he died, he changed his mind and said he'd like to have one white rose and one red rose on his coffin. He didn't know what Divine Mercy was, he'd never heard of it but here he wanted a white and red rose and when I saw that on the coffin I knew God was being merciful to him.

[Chris] In this country Alan I think when people come tonight and tomorrow and they approach you throughout your entire visit here they're seeking some type of healing. They may be thinking it's a physical healing, maybe that healing of fears. In this country one of the biggest businesses that has just exploded over the last several years and makes tons and tons of money is the business of storage units. In this country we have homes that can't contain all of the stuff that we continue to accumulate in a never ending quest to try to satisfy something, to try to medicate ourselves with things.

[Alan] I encourage anyone who has storage units and have furniture or whatever in there, give it away you don't need it, give it those who need it. There are plenty of poor people, 30 million poor people in the USA, give it to them. If there's something like St. Vincent de Paul society who give out things to the poor, give it to them. Why hold onto something you don't need or what you have to store. Of course your family photographs and things like that you keep but anything else you don't need, give it away and it's in that giving truly you can show love and help others. It is easy to get trapped in things and there's never enough. You just want more and more, you can end up with 2 or 3 storages and what do you do with it? Do you go and sit in your storage unit and look at what you've got and think isn't this wonderful, I've got all these things stored? It's much better to think it's wonderful I've given all these things away and I'm helping someone by the grace of God.

Getting back to the healings, there are many physical healings when I pray with people, there have been thousands around the world and of course it's not me, it's God that does it. We always have a Mass first before the talks because it's Jesus in the Eucharist who does the healing and we have confession and it's through confession that healing happens as well and my prayers are just a small part of the evening. There are many, many physical healings. There is one TV report that's on my website (alan-ames.org) from San Antonio, Texas, of a woman who was in a wheelchair for more than 20 years, she had a lot of other problems as well. The doctors had given up on her. I prayed with her and God healed her immediately and a big news report was done on it and she can walk, she got up out of the wheelchair. Her other physiological problems were all healed as well and she lives a perfectly healthy life now and I thank God for that.

Also, it's interesting that at the same time in San Antonio on another night they brought a young boy along who had one leg which was about 3 to 4 inches shorter than the other. The mother and grandmother brought him along and I prayed over him and as I did the leg grew in front of all the church and the legs became the same size in length. Again, they did a news report on it but they unfortunately didn't report properly so it doesn't tell the whole story but every time I go to San Antonio they bring the boy along. He's about 12 years old now and his legs are completely normal.

That's the power of God. He can do anything. He will heal you in the way that's best for you. With that boy He healed him at a young age and now his whole life he is going to be remembering God healed him. Also, what it did was to strengthen the faith throughout the whole family because they all saw the power of God and His love and now the whole family have come back to God, have come closer to God through the healing of that boy. That's what healings are all about, it's showing the love of God and the healing power of God.

[Bruce] Alan I think maybe where our hearts should be, going to these services and obviously there will be people seeking healings both physical and probably more importantly spiritually because in the end that's really what's going to matter. But I think everyone's frame of mind should be in there in their hearts, just the phrase "Thy will be done."

[Alan] I always say to people that they shouldn't come demanding from God, that whatever God wants to give, accept. It's good if you can prepare as well by saying a few prayers before you come along, but just say "Whatever you want Lord, I accept."

It's interesting as well because you can stand in for other people and they receive the prayers and often there's healings for people who don't even turn up for the talk but that someone stood in for them. Also, sometimes what happens when people are standing in for others, the person standing in is healed. I've had many letters from people who said that they went along to my talk and didn't come for themselves but for their father, or uncle, or brother, or their husband who wouldn't or couldn't come but they came to stand in for them. Well they were healed but at the same time the person standing in for them was healed. Maybe they had a bad back or bad knee, and it was all gone and they were healed because in love they opened their hearts to God. They were sacrificing for others, not thinking of themselves and their own pain but offering everything for the one they loved, in love, through the love of God, and then God healed them as well; a wonderful blessing.

[Bruce] Indeed.

[Chris] **Today's reading for the Mass is the one where the Jewish officials were essentially asking Jesus to show them a sign like Moses. Because they were anticipating the Messiah in some circles that He would bring manna as Moses did as Jesus said that Moses didn't bring the manna, it was God who provided the manna and then He says that "I am the bread of life." He is saying essentially He has sent Me, you need to turn to Me and ultimately that's the goal isn't it?**

[Alan] Yes, the Eucharist is actually the centre of our faith and it should be the centre of every Christian's faith. This is God Himself giving Himself unconditionally in love to us. When I look at John:6 which is ignored by many people in different branches of Christianity and when I see those who don't believe in the Eucharist, who turn away from the Eucharist even though Jesus has commanded us in Holy Scripture, he tells us that this is His body and His blood and unless you eat of it and drink of it you shall not have life within you. At the Last Supper He commands us to do this in memory of Him. St. Paul in Holy Scripture says those who eat unworthily of the body of Jesus and drink of His blood unworthily are liable to condemnation but if it were just bread and wine why would you be liable to condemnation?

In John 6 I always think about the many who turned away then, they couldn't accept it, it was too hard for them to believe or to understand, they turned away and left Him. He then asked the apostles and asked if they wanted to leave too, and of course the apostles said no and that's the Catholic faith today, there were many who didn't leave. There are many who did leave and in the Protestant church today they are like the ones who did leave, who left because they can't believe it, they can't accept it. It's a shame because in the Protestant churches they say they live to Holy Scripture and it's there plainly in Holy Scripture. Why can't they accept that? They accept other things in Holy Scripture, why can't they accept the exact words of Jesus and then St. Paul, the great saint who is telling us that this is the body and blood of Jesus. Yet we can make many excuses, we turn away and the ones who are doing that are turning their back on Jesus and don't believe and don't accept the fullness of Him. They remind me of the Jews in Scripture that did the same thing.

One of my prayers is that every branch of Christianity will be united in the Eucharist and accept the truth of Jesus in the Eucharist because without that truly you're not living the faith that Jesus gave us. The Eucharist is the faith of Christ, everything comes from the Eucharist, everything is in the Eucharist. It leads you to everything else because there is God who leads you to the fullness of His truth and just because we can't understand that it doesn't mean it's not true. It comes back to pride again because you look and see bread and wine and think that's not the body and blood of Jesus, how can it be? It's bread and wine. That's because we're looking with human and worldly eyes, and we're not looking beyond into the mystical into the spiritual which opens you up to show you truly that it is the body, blood, soul and divinity of Jesus Christ, Our Lord.

It's again the same thing, if we don't understand it, we can't see it, it's not tangible, we don't believe in it. That's the worldly way and I hope I don't upset our Protestant brothers and sisters because I know many wonderful Protestants who try to live their faith as best as they can. Many Protestants have a better faith than some Catholics, believe me, but many don't believe in this and because of this they don't have the fullness of faith and they don't live fully as Christ calls them to. I pray that they'll come to know the Eucharist because without that their faith is a worldly faith and that's the big mistake that Luther made, he brought the focus away from God, onto the world and onto self. If you study Luther and his life it's so obvious and I encourage all our Protestant brothers and sisters and also all Catholics to study the life of Luther, see what he said and what he did. Then you'll see that clearly it takes the focus from God and onto self and onto the world. I just hope and pray that everyone will bring the focus back onto God in heaven and the spiritual and mystical side of our faith.

[Chris] It always surprises me Alan sometimes when I see again, and it's an observation, just because I'm not Protestant but when I see on TV these huge healing services where they fill stadiums and maybe in some cases true healings do occur. Yet it is so clear in Scripture and just the experience that even those healings don't amount to the same force of grace that we experience in the Eucharist. Yet even as Catholics we don't appreciate just what an extraordinary occurrence the Eucharist provides for us if we are open to it.

[Alan] Again, it's because we're focused on the world and self and not truly focused on God. If you focus on

God in the Eucharist then you're open completely to that truth and you're lifted beyond the world, you're lifted up to levels of grace you couldn't imagine. It's way beyond this world and that's what the great mystics in the church have experienced in the Eucharist. They're lifted beyond the world, drawn up to heaven, drawn close to God and opened to the fullness of His eternal truth. That's all there in the Eucharist because in the Eucharist there is the eternal moment where, when you receive Jesus, in that moment, where God and man unite, you can experience His eternal love. His love which lifts you beyond the physical, beyond the emotional to experience the fullness of truth, the fullness of love, the fullness of eternity. In the Eucharist is everything for us.

But you're talking about the healings at these big meetings, Jesus will heal through anyone, anyone can pray for healing. The important thing for Jesus is to do the best for the person you're praying for or who is in need. So anyone who will pray in the name of Jesus and do it with a heart that's trying to love God in the best way or even sometimes those who don't love God but who are praying maybe for other reasons, Jesus looks beyond that. What He's looking at is the person who is in need and so he'll reach out and touch the person who is in need because those who come for healing are open. They're looking for Jesus, they want that healing and so He'll use that to reach out and heal them. So it doesn't surprise me that there's healing in other churches when they call on the name of Jesus because He wants the best for everyone and He'll use every opportunity to touch people in whatever way He can with the goodness of His love.

[Chris] Another opportunity for Catholics is there are many of those who truly love the Eucharist. They will always make sure that they can get to Mass when there's the opportunity to do that. Yet even for some of them the opportunity to be healed in the Sacrament of Reconciliation, which is considered one of the Sacraments of healing, why is it that that is such a stumbling block for so many?

[Alan] Well, confession, again it's down to pride isn't it because the worldly faiths have made us think we don't need to come to God for forgiveness or through the Sacrament, we can just ask God for forgiveness and that's enough. Of course it isn't. They point to the "Our Father" saying well you're asking for forgiveness there. Well in the "Our Father" the Lord is saying to us that yes, you have to come to God for forgiveness to forgive us our sins. However, when Jesus said to the apostles: "Whose sins you forgive they are forgiven...what you bind on earth is bound in heaven," He was giving the power of God to the priests, saying you have the power to forgive.

St. Peter, when he was given the authority to "bind on earth what's bound in heaven," if he said that the priests could forgive sins and no one else can, then that's bound in heaven. He also passed his authority onto the next pope and so it's passed on and if any of the popes have said that only priests can forgive sins and we must come to the priest for forgiveness of our sins, it's bound in heaven and it doesn't matter what people believe. If you don't believe that, it doesn't change that truth, that's bound in heaven. Jesus said, what's bound on earth is bound in heaven and we should remember that.

Many people don't come to confession because first of all maybe they're ashamed of themselves and the things they've done and they think I don't want to tell this man, he'll know everything about me. Of course they forget about the grace of the Holy Spirit where the priest is often helped to forget a lot of these things. Also, Satan works on our pride to try and stop us from confessing because when we hold onto sin we hold on to a weakness on our soul, there's a stain there, which is like a doorway to evil that invites evil in. This allows evil into our lives to lead us into more and more sin, further away from God.

Many people don't come to confession and it's a shame because it's such a powerful sacrament. It's pride that keeps us from confession, it's humility that leads us to it. Our Lord is the humble Lord of love and we're meant in imitation of Him to be humble, we're meant to open our heart to God. That's what we're doing when we go to confession, we're not opening our heart to the priest, we're opening our heart to God through the priest. Then God, in love, opens His heart to us and pours out the Holy Spirit which, through the powerful sacrament of the priesthood, cleanses and heals the soul when you have a full and true confession. Then when the soul is cleansed and healed it's natural that other healings would follows.

Confession is a powerful healing sacrament and sadly many people don't find healing because they don't come to confession and they hold onto their sin and so they hold onto the pain, hurt and suffering that comes with sin. Today I think it's so foolish so many people are going to psychologists, therapists and all sorts of things, paying heaps of money to go and discuss their problems in life, many of them only need to have a good confession. It's free, God doesn't charge you anything. You go in, you open your heart and you allow the Holy Spirit to fill you. You may have to go several times because you've got many things to confess. As you go more and more that grace fills you more and more, it heals you, brings peace, brings comfort and it brings your life back into order as the Holy Spirit cleanses and heals your soul, purifies you, draws you closer to God and fills you with grace. Today the evil one laughs at so many who don't believe in confession, who don't go to confession, who hold onto their sins, hold onto their pride and so make it easier for the evil one to draw them away from God.

[Bruce] Alan, we really need to know just as Christ is really present in the Eucharist, as our priests act in persona Christi, as the person of Christ, not only at the altar. They are also doing so in the confessional and as they administer all the sacraments of the church.

[Alan] It's true. There's Christ in every priest and God gives them such grace, it's beyond anything any other person can achieve. Through the sacrament of the priesthood the power of the Holy Spirit is incredible and in confession is the power to cleanse and heal souls. It's not the power of the priest, it's the power of the priesthood which is given by Christ and bestowed in wonderful love on the man who becomes a priest. Only a man as a priest because truly women can't be priests and I know people say you've got to have equal rights but God gives us a way to live and He gives us equal rights. Men and women are equal in His eyes but we have different roles and one of the roles for a man is to be a priest and it's through the man as a priest that Christ then pours out this grace. The grace of the power of the Holy Spirit to cleanse and heal souls and to bring your life to fullness in Him and to draw you closer to Him. It's so important we have a good confession but sadly so many people don't believe that.

[Bruce] I know that...certainly as we go, hardly anyone that comes out of confession. When it's done you finally go Oh, I'm glad I got that load off of my heart. It is a feeling that, it's almost indescribable, that forgiveness that God loves you that much.

[Alan] I often meet people who haven't been to confession for 20 or 30 years. They go to confession and come out crying saying why didn't I do this before. I say yes, why didn't you?

[Chris] Exactly. It struck me too when you were talking about the priesthood, we have to remember that the sacrament of holy orders is a gift to the church and that for the priests they are still men. They are still a human being but yet their character has changed by the imposition of the hands and the calling on of the Holy Spirit. I think, Alan, so often throughout the world and maybe in America moreso because we have the rugged individual and the business model and we end up looking at the priest as though he's just another leader in the Church as opposed to that person who stands in for us as a conduit to Christ.

[Bruce] He's given his life for that.

[Chris] Yes, exactly. I think that is a struggle for so many when they think about the Eucharist because we've lost that sense and maybe Satan laughs at that because we no longer pray for the priest. We just get mad at him because he's not what we expect, or want him to be.

[Alan] Again, it's all about I, what I want, what I expect and we forget also the sacrifices the priest makes. They make so many sacrifices, giving their whole life for Christ, doing it publicly, openly and they come under so much attack. We should be supporting the priests because truly they are great, great blessings but sadly today so many attack the priests. It's a weakness of faith because what it shows is that we no longer are seeing Christ in the priesthood, we're not placing the importance on holy orders that we should.

Many Catholics do that even those who go to daily Mass. If you ask people have you mentioned to your son about being a priest, most say no, they want their sons to be lawyers, doctors, accountants, on the stock markets, to make big money. It's all worldly stuff. It's all about the world and these are many devout Catholics who go to church but they don't talk to their sons about being priests or their daughters about being nuns because the religious life is not seen as that good a job or that important and yet they profess to be good Catholics. Every Catholic should be talking to their children about holy orders and helping them to maybe decide to be a priest or a religious. If they don't want to be, that's fine but if they want to be we should be helping them and encouraging them but if we don't talk to them about a vocation they won't even think about it.

Today so many Catholics say we haven't got that many priests and I say, why? it's because we're not talking to our children about being priests and being nuns. We're seeing it as less important and we don't realize that this is a great treasure, full of grace, full of gifts, full of love. Instead we're thinking about the jobs that bring money, fame, prestige, importance in the world and again that's the worldly way, the secular way and how the evil one laughs.

[Chris] Before we close I have to ask this opportunity that we have in the US right now. It's a tremendous time of grace with the Holy Father coming, and of course magazines throughout the country, the secular institutions, are trying to show us, well here are all the problems he's encountering or here are all the issues with the church. Do you have a word for us in America about the fact that we have this great theologian who does theology really on his knees in prayer?

[Alan] I think he's a great pope. John Paul II was a fantastic Pope, wonderful, very spiritual, very mystical. Now this is the plan of God, he's brought the next Pope along who is different but so holy, so wonderful, so strong, and so gentle and if you look his whole life is about love, love of God. Everything he talks about is love and he doesn't care too much about what the secular say about him and what people think about him, he just cares about people.

He cares about loving God and imitating Christ, being the shepherd of the flock and it doesn't matter what the secular world say and do. God's grace will reach through the Pope and touch people in this country and draw them to the fullness of God's truth. He's a wonderful pope we should be praying for him and I hope he stays with us a while because he's certainly bringing our focus onto many things that we haven't looked at and we should be looking at and helping us to reach out more to God in love. He's a great blessing for the world and I thank God for him.

[Bruce] I'm sure he'll have some very frank things to say to us here in America and we're looking forward to him. Alan thank you so much for being generous with your time. We'll pray that sleep comes in great quantities for you here as you continue a very busy schedule saying yes in the most wonderful way to the Lord's calling to you.

[Alan] Thank you very much Bruce and Chris and everyone in Omaha. Please pray for me, I'll pray for you.

Books available from:

USA

Alan Ames Ministry
PO Box 200
233 Glasgow Avenue SW
Kellogg
Minnesota 55945

Phone: 507 767 3027
Web: http://www.alanames.org

Australia

Touch of Heaven
(Alan Ames Ministry)
PO Box 85
Wembley, 6014
West Australia

Phone: 61 89275 6608
Fax: 61 89382 4392
Web: http://www.alanames.ws
Email: touchofheaven@iinet.net.au